NATIONAL WILDLIFE'S
DECEMBER TREASURY

Library of Congress CIP Data: page 191

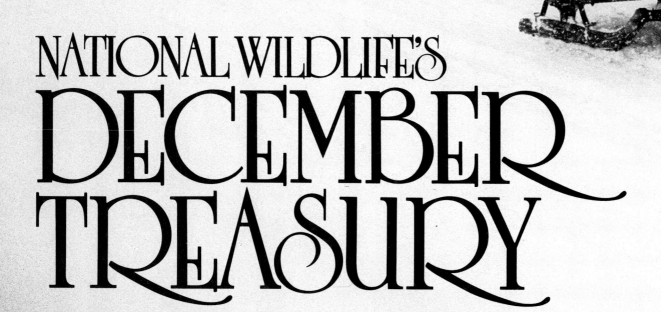

NATIONAL WILDLIFE'S
DECEMBER TREASURY

December may be the last page on our calendar, but it belongs to no single year. This is a special, magical season, ruled less by time than by age-old traditions, the echoes of warm memories, and the joy of the holidays. For all of us, December is a month-long holiday celebration.

Now we bring in the Christmas tree; now we gather boughs of spruce and pine and sprigs of holly and mistletoe to decorate the house. And as the sharp scent of evergreens blends with the sweet aroma of family recipes, we join with friends, neighbors, and generations of our kin to share the festive spirit.

In December, nature also contributes to the wonder of the season, as winter spreads its magic all over the land. In the southern states, frost may delicately outline thousands of tree branches and etch the roadside grasses with fragile silvery threads. Farther north, from New England to the high Rockies, December snows unfold a Christmas-card scenery: skaters test newly frozen lakes while skiers check the snowpack. But no matter how much we may enjoy this fairy-tale world, sooner or later we all gladly surrender to the lure of a warm, crackling fire indoors.

Consider the warm glow of the house on our cover as an open invitation to come and share with us the pages of *December Treasury*. We searched with great care through the works of writers, artists, and photographers, and now we offer you our collection of the best classic and contemporary impressions of winter, wildlife, and holiday memories. Whether a painting by Grandma Moses or Robert Bateman, a passage by Emily Dickinson or Henry David Thoreau, we hope you will find something to cherish in the readings and images for each day of December. And as you share these pages with family and friends, perhaps *December Treasury* will become the cornerstone for your new holiday memories.

Ice skaters on a New England pond, by DeWitt Jones.

DECEMBER 1

DECEMBER

The arrival of December means the definite end to autumn. Even the leaf-rustle of the November wind whisking October's brilliance along the country road is muted as the leaves settle down. The early clamor of crows no longer starts the day, and the jays go about their business for the most part in blue silence. The chickadee is the most vocal bird in the dooryard, and his brief song is interrupted by the tap-tap-tap of his beak as he cracks a sunflower seed. In the country house, the fly-buzz and wasp-flutter in the attic have quieted down, the insects dead or dormant.

The barred owl hoots in the night, and from time to time the fine-spun yapping of a red fox is heard. But their voices only punctuate the silence, which lies deep in the rural valley where frogs, only a few weeks ago, thumped the darkness. Brooks are quiet, their shallow waters beginning to clog with ice. The woodchuck sleeps. Chipmunks drowse in their fluff-lined nests, and squirrels go chatterless in the treetops.

December comes, a time of earth sounds, the moan of the chilling wind, the swish of driven snow. Sometimes the countryman wakens in the night and thinks he hears the faint groan of rocks restless in their age-old beds, nudged by the slow expansion of silent frost. Sometimes he hears the slow crunch of ice on the pond. December comes, and winter.

—*Hal Borland, 1979*

6

"It Snows, Oh It Snows," oil painting by Grandma Moses, 1951.

THE HOUSE IN WINTER

*The house in winter creaks like a ship.
Snow-locked to the sills and harbored snug
In soft white meadows, it is not asleep.
When icicles pend on the low roof's lip,
The shifting weight of a slow-motion tug
May slide off sometimes in a crashing slip.
At zero I have heard a nail pop out
From clapboard like a pistol shot.*

*All day this ship is sailing out on light:
At dawn we wake to rose and amber meadows,
At noon plunge on across the waves of white,
And, later, when the world becomes too bright,
Tack in among the lengthening blue shadows
To anchor in black-silver pools of night.
Although we do not really come and go,
It feels a long way up and down from zero.*

*At night I am aware of life aboard.
The scampering presences are often kind,
Leaving under a cushion a seed-hoard,
But I can never open any cupboard
Without a question: what shall I find?
A hard nut in my boot? An apple cored?
The house around me has become an ark
As we go creaking on from dark to dark.*

*There is a wilder solitude in winter
When every sense is pricked alive and keen
For what may pop or tumble down or splinter.
The light itself, as active as a painter,
Swashes bright flowing banners down
The flat white walls. I stand here like a hunter
On the* qui vive, *though all appears quite calm,
And feel the silence gather like a storm.*

—May Sarton, 1966

9

WINTER NEIGHBORS

The country is more of a wilderness, more of a wild solitude, in the winter than in the summer. The wild comes out. The urban, the cultivated, is hidden or negatived. You shall hardly know a good field from a poor, a meadow from a pasture, a park from a forest. The best-kept grounds relapse to a state of nature; under the pressure of the cold all the wild creatures become outlaws, and roam abroad beyond their usual haunts. The partridge comes to the orchard for buds; the rabbit comes to the garden and lawn; the crows and jays come to the ash-heap and corn-crib, the snow-buntings to the stack and to the barn-yard; the sparrows pilfer from the domestic fowls; the pine grosbeak comes down from the north and shears your maples of their buds; the red squirrels find your grain in the barn or steal the butternuts from your attic. In fact, winter, like some great calamity, changes the status of most creatures and sets them adrift. Winter, like poverty, makes us acquainted with strange bedfellows.

For my part, my nearest approach to a strange bedfellow is the little gray rabbit that has taken up her abode under my study floor. As she spends the day here and is out larking at night, she is not much of a bedfellow after all. It is probable that I disturb her slumbers more than she does mine. I think she is some support to me under there—a silent wild-eyed witness and backer; a type of the gentle and harmless in savage nature. She has no sagacity to give me or lend me, but that soft, nimble foot of hers, and that touch as of cotton wherever she goes, are worthy of emulation. I think I can feel her good-will through the floor, and I hope she can mine. When I have a happy thought I imagine her ears twitch, especially when I think of the sweet apple I will place by her doorway at night.

—*John Burroughs, 1886*

Winter, like poverty, makes us acquainted with strange bedfellows.

— ❋ —

Winter neighbors: flying squirrel (far left), by Stephen J. Krasemann; deer mouse (top left), by John Gerlach; pine grosbeak (above), by Stephen J. Krasemann; and cottontail (left), by Karl Maslowski.

DECEMBER 2

FROST-WORK

These winter nights, against my window-pane
Nature with busy pencil draws designs
Of ferns and blossoms and fine spray of pines,
Oak-leaf and acorn and fantastic vines,
Which she will make when summer comes again—
Quaint arabesques in argent, flat and cold,
Like curious Chinese etchings....By and by,
Walking my leafy garden as of old,
These frosty fantasies shall charm my eye
In azure, damask, emerald, and gold.

     —Thomas Bailey Aldrich, 1882

A ghostly figure (left) peers through a frosted window, by Brian Milne. Detail of hoarfrost on a windowpane (right), by R. Y. Kaufman.

WINTER'S ICY LACEWORK

So frost is on the land at last, the stiff rime of
it dusted across the grass, treacherous on the
stones, exquisite along each vein of the
leached-out skeleton leaf. Frost is in the golden
crown of that beggar king, the dandelion; frost
pushes up out of the red clay in a gleaming forest
of curving icicles, so strong that it has lifted the
earth and even little stones high on its cold
prongs, so frail that at a touch of my cane I can
slay it as easily as so many glass flowers. Sickles
and spirals and curls like a carpenter's shavings
are shooting out of the stems of the frostweed,
and from the dittany, which has the same odd
property of extruding the water in its stem.

—*Donald Culross Peattie, 1935*

So frost is on the land at last, . . . exquisite along each vein
of the leached-out skeleton leaf.

— ❄ —

Frost decorates milkweed pods
(far left), by John Shaw; winter-
berries (left), by Larry West;
and maple leaves (above), by
Tom and Pat Leeson.

FROST FACTS

❄ Frost forms when the earth's temperature falls below 32°F and water vapor in the atmosphere freezes as it descends toward the earth's surface. The crystals trace the outlines of houses, rocks, and plants with icy lace.

❄ Hoarfrost is the aggregation of icy crystals that forms patterns of feathers or scales on windowpanes.

❄ Valleys are particularly susceptible to frost: The heavy cold air from the surrounding highlands descends to the valleys, coating them with frost.

DECEMBER 3

A SHARING OF PERSIMMONS

There are fifteen or twenty persimmon trees scattered across the hilly sweep of pasture land, most of them low and picturesquely grouped around outcroppings of gray, lichen-covered granite. In the spring their glossy, deep green leaves sparkle in the sunlight and obscure the small white blossoms that droop along the twigs and smaller branches. In the fall the long leathery leaves gleam a bright orange-red and hide the unripe fruits that hang from the same stiff calyces that held the springtime blossoms.

When the all-concealing leaves drop to the ground the nakedness of these trees is not quite complete, for each one clutches a multitude of orange-brown fruits in its multitude of twiggy fingers. And when winter's bitter weather arrives, each little fruit left still swinging in the wind is a flavorful bite of persimmon frappé.

And I love persimmon frappé. I love persimmons. Persimmons just ripe enough to be eaten. Persimmons soft and squashy and overripe. Persimmons cold and frosted with ice. Persimmons wrinkled and thawed and almost liquid with age.

Most persimmon trees carry their fruits high in their crowns, teasing and tantalizing, while their lower branches hang bare. But these trees load their lower branches just as prodigally as they fill their crowns, and I feast from October through December, and sometimes into the first months of the new year, with only an occasional leap to pull a higher branch down to picking level.

Only once or twice in half a dozen years, to my knowledge, has another human being picked any of the luscious fruit; but the crop is not left entirely, nor even mostly, to me.

There is a battle-happy mockingbird who tries to control all twenty trees, and he flies himself ragged in his efforts to drive winged poachers from his far-flung domain. He does an astoundingly good job of it, too, probably because the area is so open and because most birds would rather fly than fight.

I saw him outwitted, though, one December day, by a flock of fifteen cedar waxwings who, after being chased from one tree to another for almost an hour, simply split into three small groups, flew low over the snow-covered ground, and came up into the trees undetected.

Once they started to rip open his precious fruits, the mockingbird saw them and pounced upon them, but he could only harass one small group at a time, and all the cedar waxwings managed to stuff themselves with persimmons.

A raccoon plucks ripe persimmons, by K. Maslowski.

...a battle-happy mockingbird...flies himself ragged in his efforts to drive winged poachers from his far-flung domain.

— ❄ —

Persimmons on the tree are food for the birds, and fallen ones are quickly scooped up by the resident foxes, skunks, raccoons and opossums. There are hollow trees complete with raccoons in the nearby woods, a lived-in fox den among the rocks in the ravine, and at least three groundhog holes right there in the pasture.

From the fox den to the persimmon trees I find only fox tracks; but from the groundhog holes the tracks of opossums and the dainty prints of skunks make single-minded pathways directly to the trees—and wide-wandering, notional meanderings on the return trip to warmth and darkness.

Raccoons come from the woods most often, but sometimes I find the track of a raccoon mingled with the others on the pathways between the persimmon trees and the groundhog holes, and then I know that yet another spare bedspace in groundhog lodgings is occupied by a needy sojourner. The groundhog is sound asleep in his own sealed-off bedchamber and he does not know and does not care who takes refuge in his outer burrow.

I have never seen a raccoon eating a persimmon, although I know they do, but once I did find one up the tree. Or perhaps he found me. It was early in the morning of another December day, not stormy, but cold and clear, with an inch of new snow on the ground, all soft and fluffy and marked with the mingled tracks of neighborhood animals. I did not realize that more tracks led to the tree than led away from it.

With the tree at my back and Kela, my dog, at my side I stood tiptoe and plucked a frozen persimmon from an outer branch. I bit through thin tissue skin into sweet icy pulp, closed my eyes to savor its frosty flavor, and felt the force of staring eyes on the back of my neck. I looked uneasily over my shoulder but saw no one. Kela was undisturbed, so I went back to my eating.

The feeling of being watched continued and, though Kela remained perfectly calm, I grew increasingly uneasy and finally turned around so that I faced the direction from which the staring seemed to come. But still I saw no one.

Something made me look into the tree and there was a young raccoon about six feet above me. He was leaning against the trunk and surveying me steadily, with bright and curious eyes, through his dark burglar's mask.

Persimmons and opossums go together just as naturally as love and marriage are supposed to, so quite often I find an opossum or two perched in one of the trees. Whether they are ignoring Kela and me or whether their primitive little brains just do not register our presence I have never been able to decide, but they go on with their eating as though we did not exist, and I am glad that it is so. To watch, and to hear, an opossum eating a persimmon is a vicarious experience in the absolutely uninhibited joy of eating.

The opossum perches himself comfortably somewhere in the crown of the tree in easy reaching distance of several persimmons. He clings to the branches with his bare pink feet and hooks his hairless gray tail over the limb behind him for balance. Then he dreamily closes his eyelids over his round dark eyes, and, with the fifty teeth in his shallow jaws, he chops one delectable fruit after another in a lip-smacking, saliva-spattering, juice-slobbering ecstasy.

—*Mary Leister, 1976*

A mockingbird stands watch over its territory, by Leonard Lee Rue III.

AH, PERSIMMONS!

A young opossum scans the woods from a lofty perch, by Gerald Wiens.

❀ Persimmon trees are found throughout the eastern half of the United States, except in the extreme north. Unripe, the fruit is terribly bitter, but when it ripens after the first frost, it becomes soft and sweet. The plumlike fruit hangs on the trees well into winter, providing food for songbirds, turkey, deer, and many other mammals and birds.

❀ In the South, Indians sometimes dried and ground the fruits to make bread. The seeds were also roasted and used as a substitute for coffee.

❀ The high sugar content in persimmons makes the fruit a versatile kitchen ingredient. The pulp has been used to concoct edibles from molasses, beer, and vinegar to cookies, bread, and pudding.

Persimmon Pudding

2 cups persimmon pulp
1 cup sugar
1 egg
2 cups milk
2 cups flour
1 teaspoon soda
½ tsp. salt
1 tsp. cinnamon
½ tsp. cloves
½ tsp. allspice

Combine the ingredients, beating well. It is best to save about half the milk until all the flour has been added. Pour about 1½ inches deep in well greased pans; bake at 325° for about an hour. The pudding turns dark brown when done. Serve warm or cold with whipped cream.

Adapted from *Edible Wild Plants of Eastern North America*, by Merritt L. Fernald and Alfred C. Kinsey

Persimmon Bread

1 cup persimmon pulp, with seeds removed
1 egg beaten into ½ cup milk
1 tbsp. melted margarine or butter
1 cup sugar
1½ cups flour
½ tsp. salt
1 tsp. baking powder
1 tsp. soda
½ tsp. cinnamon

Mix the persimmon pulp, egg, milk, and melted margarine. Add the sifted dry ingredients and mix well. Place in a loaf pan and bake at 325° for 1 hour or until it springs back when touched lightly with the finger. Serve sliced with butter, or plain.

Persimmon Cookies

½ cup shortening
1 cup sugar
1 egg
2 cups flour
1 tsp. soda
pinch salt
½ tsp. each, cinnamon, nutmeg, and cloves
1 cup persimmon pulp
1 cup nuts
1 cup raisins

Cream shortening and sugar; add egg, then add flour, soda, salt, and spices, alternating with persimmon pulp; mix well. Add nuts and raisins and mix to incorporate. Batter should be quite stiff. Drop by teaspoonfuls onto cookie sheets. Bake at 350° until light brown on top.

Adapted from *Wild Fruits: An Illustrated Guide and Cookbook*, by Mildred Fielder.

DECEMBER 4

WINTER SLEEPERS

Time now for the long sleep of the four-footed brethren. The frosty nights, the days so brief and so subdued, the cold and voiceless emptiness of the ruined woods, have warned the woodchucks, the pine mice, the chipmunks and the bats. And now in couples, or in families, they creep away to their lairs.

When I am troubled with insomnia, I think not upon those foolish sheep, jumping heavily and wearily over a stile. I think instead of the sleep of the white-footed mice, in their burrows and hollows, warm flank to warm flank, clever little paws folded over sensitive noses and whiskers, as they doze away the days and the nights together, secure in their retreat, contented with their lot. They sleep as the plants sleep in their roots and bulbs. Their hearts beat so slowly that they scarce suffice to force the warm blood through the chilled limbs; minds are a blank, all hunger, desires, impulses and fears in abeyance for days and days, for weeks and weeks. So do these little fellows sleep, five and ten at a time, fallen upon each other in little furry windrows of drowsiness.

—Donald Culross Peattie, 1935

— ❋ —

Scientists researching hibernation kept a hibernating ground squirrel for their studies. The squirrel slept so soundly that the scientists were able to toss it back and forth like a ball without disturbing its slumber.

Curled up in a warm ball, a golden-mantled ground squirrel sleeps for the winter, by Jeff Foott.

A SNOWDRIFT DEN

One of the unforgettable experiences of a friend happened when he was cross-country skiing in the woods a few miles from our house. He noticed an odd snowdrift beneath the base of an uprooted tree. The surface of the drift was honeycombed with peculiar, almost hexagonal, patches of snow. Curious, he poked his ski pole at the largest patch, about six inches in diameter.

At once the cracks between all the patches widened. One edge of the snowdrift crumbled away, revealing a clump of heavy black moss. Then, to my friend's astonishment, the "moss" blinked and turned in his general direction.

That was all the information my friend needed. The strange snowdrift, it turned out, was the body of a slumbering bear. The snow had assumed the honeycomb texture because of the slight bit of warmth that penetrated through the fur. And, when the bear had been prodded, its involuntary intake of breath caused the patches to separate from each other.

Although the black bear normally shuns contact with humans, there was no telling what this creature would do when it found itself face to face with an intruder. The question remains unanswered, however. Befogged by sleep, the bear's bleary eyes failed to discern the skier, who stood as though rooted to the spot. Its keen sense of smell failed to pick out any unusual scent, either. The animal returned to its nap while my friend, who said his heart was pounding so hard he was sure it would wake the bear again, waited five minutes before setting a new woodland cross-country ski record.

—*Ronald Rood, 1973*

FOOD FOR THE WINTER

[Bears] will Sleep so soundly for fourteen Days that it is not possible by any means to awaken them, and...during their abode in those secret Places, they never appear abroad for Food, but only suck their Paws, which is all they subsist upon during that time.

—*John Brickell, 1737*

BEARS' WINTER MUSIC

When [bears] take up their winter-quarters, they continue the greater part of two months, in almost an entire state of inactivity....While they are employed in that surprising task of nature, they cannot contain themselves in silence, but are so well pleased with their repast, that they continue singing *hum um um:* as their pipes are none of the weakest, the Indians by this means often are led to them from a considerable distance, and then shoot them down.

—*James Adair, 1775*

. . . during their abode in those secret Places, they . . . only suck their
Paws, which is all they subsist upon . . . .

— ❈ —

Stories crediting bears with feeding themselves through their winter sleep by sucking on their paws are found in almost every culture which has come into contact with the creatures. In the Winnebago Indian version of the story, bears spend their summer walking on berries, crushing the different fruits with their paws. Come winter, all they have to do is lick their paws to obtain the essence of berry.

According to Lynn Rogers, a biologist who has been closely studying bears for more than a decade, bears do, indeed, lick their paws while they rest in their winter dens. The explanation, however, has more to do with comfort than sustenance. Their hard foot pads flake off during hibernation, and the bears are left with tender feet. They lick their feet to soothe them.

As to the bruins' winter serenade, science supports the folklore. Bears not only hum, they hum loudly. "I've heard it from a blind located sixty yards from the den.

On a calm day, I think it could be easily heard at twice that distance," says Rogers.

But the sound doesn't come from adult bears; it's a cub choir. Apparently, whenever they are warm, comfortable, and feeling good about life, bear cubs will hum in self-satisfaction. In the course of his research on denning bears, Rogers has cradled cubs while they contentedly hummed in his arms.

— ❈ —

Entrance to a bear's den (opposite), by Tom Bean. Snug inside a den, a mother bear and cub sleep out the winter (below), by Lynn Rogers.

A well-furred arctic fox waits out a blizzard, by R. Hamilton Smith.

Hibernation is only one effective strategy in nature for surviving the cold. Rather than sleeping through the worst of the cold, some creatures are wonderfully designed to grin and bear it—the arctic fox is among the best equipped. Most of its fur is made up of fine, warm underfur. This winter coat is so toasty that the fox will not begin to shiver until the temperature dips to -60°F. During severe storms, the fox will tunnel into a snowbank to wait out the blizzard.

BEATING THE CHILL

Sleeping it Off

❋ Contrary to popular belief, no creature in nature sleeps continuously throughout the winter. Even deep hibernators such as woodchucks and ground squirrels will wake up for occasional brief spells. Lighter sleepers such as bears can wake up completely if disturbed.

❋ The meadow jumping mouse, a widespread rodent throughout the northern half of North America, spends more than half its life in hibernation.

❋ The only hibernating bird in the world is the common poorwill. This member of the nightjar family breeds from southeastern British Columbia down to central Mexico and overwinters from the southwestern United States down into Mexico. Hibernating poorwills have been found only in California and Arizona.

❋ With the exception of bats, all hibernating mammals curl into a tight ball for their winter sleep. Those with bushy tails wrap them over their backs; those with naked tails tuck their tails next to their toasty abdomens.

Built-In Antifreeze

❋ For some insects, surviving the cold means to winterize. Many insects that live in areas of cold winters secrete glycol into their bodies. Glycol is similar to the antifreeze we use to winterize our cars.

A Winter Coat

❋ Caribou, moose, deer, and elk hair is hollow, trapping warmth against the animals' bodies.

❋ Even the caribou's muzzle is furred; as the animal thrusts it into the snow to find food, the muzzle stays warm.

❋ Tree squirrels must compromise in winter. They need warmth, but their lives must still be carried on in the trees where a heavy winter coat might steal some of their agility. In winter, squirrels' fur grows only a little fuller around the body and very full on the tail. If it gets too nippy, a squirrel wraps its tail around its nose to take the edge off the chill.

❋ Musk ox and caribou also make use of communal warmth. Members of a herd stand in close ranks and warm each other. In addition, the combined breath of the closely packed individuals forms a cloud of vapor that traps warm air from their bodies.

27

DECEMBER 5

THE WOOD-PILE

Out walking in the frozen swamp one grey day,
I paused and said, 'I will turn back from here.
No, I will go on farther—and we shall see.'
The hard snow held me, save where now and then
One foot went through. The view was all in lines
Straight up and down of tall slim trees
Too much alike to mark or name a place by
So as to say for certain I was here
Or somewhere else: I was just far from home.
A small bird flew before me. He was careful
To put a tree between us when he lighted,
And say no word to tell me who he was
Who was so foolish as to think what he *thought.*
He thought that I was after him for a feather—
The white one in his tail; like one who takes
Everything said as personal to himself.
One flight out sideways would have undeceived him.
And then there was a pile of wood for which
I forgot him and let his little fear
Carry him off the way I might have gone,
Without so much as wishing him good-night.
He went behind it to make his last stand.
It was a cord of maple, cut and split
And piled—and measured, four by four by eight.
And not another like it could I see.
No runner tracks in this year's snow looped near it.
And it was older sure than this year's cutting,
Or even last year's or the year's before.
The wood was grey and the bark warping off it
And the pile somewhat sunken. Clematis
Had wound strings round and round it like a bundle.
What held it though on one side was a tree
Still growing, and on one a stake and prop,
These latter about to fall. I thought that only
Someone who lived in turning to fresh tasks
Could so forget his handiwork on which
He spent himself, the labour of his axe,
And leave it there far from a useful fireplace
To warm the frozen swamp as best it could
With the slow smokeless burning of decay.

—Robert Frost, 1914

"Gathering Wood for Winter,"
oil painting by George Henry
Durrie, 1855.

FIREWOOD OPPORTUNISTS

A flock of a dozen chickadees spends the year in my woods. In winter, when we are harvesting diseased or dead trees for our fuel wood, the ring of the axe is dinner gong for the chickadee tribe. They hang in the offing waiting for the tree to fall, offering pert commentary on the slowness of our labor. When the tree at last is down, and the wedges begin to open up its contents, the chickadees draw up their white napkins and fall to. Every slab of dead bark is, to them, a treasury of eggs, larvae, and cocoons. For them every ant-tunneled heartwood bulges with milk and honey. We often stand a fresh split against a near-by tree just to see the greedy chicks mop up the ant-eggs. It lightens our labor to know that they, as well as we, derive aid and comfort from the fragrant riches of newly split oak.

—*Aldo Leopold, 1949*

A black-capped chickadee perches on its woody dinner table (above), by John Gerlach. A trail of chimney smoke emerges from Aldo Leopold's cabin in Wisconsin (right), by Tom Algire.

30

FIRELIGHT NIGHTS

For us the pleasures of our fireplace begin even before we light the first fire. During the latter days of October and the early days of November, Nellie and I range through the woods over fallen leaves, gathering sticks, breaking up dry branches, picking up poles in a harvest of winter kindling.

Then, in the short winter days and the long winter evenings, the great fireplace of our living room comes into its own. It brings light and color and movement and sound and perfume and a direct warmth into the room where an old wall clock ticks away the minutes and chimes the hours and half-hours throughout the day and night.

The appeal of an open fireplace is deep-seated. It has its roots in four of our five senses: sight, hearing, feeling, smelling. We watch the flicker and the altering shapes and colors of the flames. We hear the snapping and crackling of the burning logs. We smell the perfume of the various woods as they are consumed. We feel the warmth of the dancing flames and glowing coals. Endlessly these elements are combined and recombined. No two fireplace fires are ever the same. Each represents a different pattern of flames, a different sequence of sounds, a different play of colors. These fires of winter are as dissimilar as wave marks on the seashore, as varied as autumn leaves or flakes of snow or human beings.

The voices of our fireplace range from a soft flutter of flames, like a silken flag flapping in the breeze, through sharp snappings of the burning wood, like small firecrackers exploding. At times there are tiny cracklings like sleet on a windowpane. Then, at the end of the evening, come the sleepy-sounding fires, dying, falling into silence with a soft simmer and murmur as lulling as rippling water or rustling leaves.

How wonderfully snug and enclosed we feel in winter storms with logs blazing on the hearth! Sitting there, gazing at the ever-changing kaleidoscope of the flames as they flicker before the smoke-blackened stones, we often become aware of a curious dislocation in time. We might be enjoying this warmth and light and color in any other period during the long history of this companionable hearth—before the first airplane flew or before the Civil War or when California was in Spanish hands. In no other hours is this feeling of temporarily being afloat in time, of living in undated moments, more apparent than when Nellie, filling in gaps in our acquaintance with the classics, reads aloud at the end of the day from books that came into being over a span of centuries of time.

And as the winter days go by, as the logs of oak and maple and hickory that are packed row on row in the center shed, each in turn burn to ashes, we watch the piles dwindle down like sand in an hourglass. Each year we burn about five cords of wood in our living-room fireplace. The gradual disappearance of our fireplace wood measures, as in some larger glass, the progress of the season. In all varieties of winter weather I bring in the logs. Often as I emerge from the shed, a log on my shoulder, the smell of woodsmoke is sweet in the clear cold air.

—*Edwin Way Teale, 1974*

A blaze in an open fireplace warms body and soul, by H. Armstrong Roberts.

Firewood Tips

❊ Ideally, firewood should be thoroughly dry and seasoned before burning. If you burn wet wood, the water turns into steam which escapes up the chimney, taking precious heat along with it.

❊ Dense wood burns more slowly and gives off more heat than light wood. Among the best firewood trees are hickory, oak, beech, and sugar maple, while evergreens and poplars yield poor firewood.

❊ Lighter woods and dead evergreen twigs light easily and burn quickly, making good kindling.

❊ For an aromatic fire, burn fruit-tree logs. Apple, pear, and black cherry wood will all give your fire a wonderful fragrance.

Old Popular Belief

If smoke from your chimney sinks to the ground, be prepared for a heavy snowfall within thirty days and a severe winter.

Every man looks at his woodpile with a kind of affection. I loved to have mine before my window, and the more chips the better to remind me of my pleasing work.

—*H. D. Thoreau*, Walden, 1854

A Drink to Sip by the Fire: Mulled Cider

¾ cup firmly packed
   brown sugar
¼ tsp. salt
1 tsp. cloves
1 tsp. allspice
3 sticks cinnamon
grated nutmeg
2 quarts sweet cider

Thoroughly mix brown sugar, salt and spices; add to sweet cider and simmer 10 minutes; strain through cheesecloth and reheat. This is best served steaming hot in earthen mugs. Serves 8.

Reprinted from *A Gift of Mistletoe*, by Elizabeth Deane

What's a Three-Dog Night?

We asked an old-time resident of Maine to set us straight on this, and here is his report.

"Well . . . up here in the wintertime, it gets kind of cold. Now . . . if you're a bachelor like myself, what you need on a seriously cold night is a little warmth. Preferably it oughta have a self-contained source of power so it won't go and get cold on you during the night (you're lookin' for an advantage here over a hot-water bottle). It should have kind of a soft pleasant aspect to it so's you can abide bein' real close, and it oughta be mobile so you can get it under the covers with you. Now I don't know what choices you people got available to you down in the big cities, but up here, about the only thing that fits the bill is the family dog.

"If it ain't too cold an evening, I might get by with, say, just that little terrier of mine curled up near my feet. But when the season really gets a grip on the country up here, I find myself being more than usually friendly to my fine young collie. I can usually coax her to take up alongside my back, and with that and the terrier at my feet, I make out O.K.

"Long about yesterday, I saw the way the temperature was fallin' and I started lookin' at this other dog I got around the place. He's a mean old critter, and I ain't paid much attention to him since he took a bite out of one of the few callers I do get up this way. But as the sun went down, he started to look a little different to me, and I gave him a good meal and commenced to pattin' on his head a little. He seemed agreeable after a while, and then I called to the other two and we settled down under the covers for the evening. And that, sir, is what we call a three-dog night."

Adapted from *The Cold Weather Catalogue*, 1977

DECEMBER 6

MOONLIGHT OWL

All too seldom do we emerge from the snugness of our hearthside into the long winter night to listen and to admire the snowy landscape. When floodlit by a moon nearly full, the snow crystals glitter and sparkle almost as brightly as the stars. It seems incredible that the brilliance at our feet comes from our own sun, now hidden from sight by the bulk of the earth, yet reflected from the distant moon. It transforms each breath we exhale into a crystal cloud, and helps us cast black shadows on the solid froth of frozen water squeaking below our feet.

A rounded lump on a low branch becomes an owl. We say nothing; neither does the bird. Great eyes blink in our direction, singly or together. Suddenly, without a sound, the owl is airborne. Through the bushes at the edge of the meadow it banks in the manner of a stunt pilot to dodge a branch. In full moonlight the trick looks easy, but the owl achieves the same silent disappearance when light is almost lacking. Now the bird swoops low over the snow and glides with great wings spread, silent as any mouse, ready to pounce on one. No mouse appears in the bird's path, and the owl rises to a new perch in a distant tree. Still there has been no sound. We are about to move on when across the field comes the voice we have waited for—the song of the owl.

—*Lorus and Margery Milne, 1963*

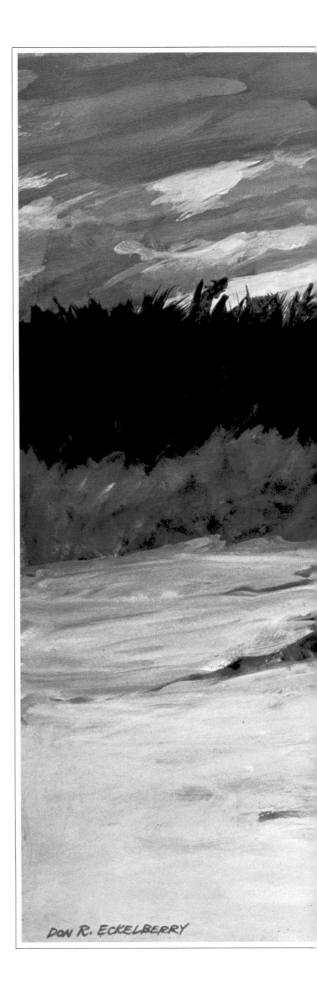

"Barn Owl—Evening Flight," acrylic painting by Don R. Eckelberry, c. 1971.

DON R. ECKELBERRY

DECEMBER MOON

The full moon of December is no summer serenader's moon, no sentimental moon of silvery softness to match the rhyming of the ballad singer. It is a winter's moon with more than fourteen hours of darkness to rule in cold splendor.

It is not a silvery moon at all. This is a moon of ice, cold and distant. But it shimmers the hills where there is a frosting of snow and it makes the frozen valleys gleam. It dances on the dark surface of an up-country pond. It weaves fantastic patterns on the snow in the woodland. It is the sharp edge of the night wind, the silent feather on the great horned owl's wing, the death-scream of an unwary rabbit when the red fox has made its pounce.

This winter's moon is a silent companion for the nightwalker, a deceptive light that challenges the eye. It dims the huddled hemlocks on the hillside, and it sharpens the hilltop horizon. It wreathes the walker's head in the shimmer of his own breath, and it seems to whistle in his footsteps. It makes wreaths of chimney smoke and sweetens the smell of the hearth-fire.

It is the long winter night in cold splendor, night wrapped in frost, spangled and sequined and remote as Arcturus.

—Hal Borland, 1979

36

Winter moonlight silhouettes the naked branches of a white ash, by John Shaw.

THE STARFIELD

All above the black line of our North Woods, the sheets of light were growing brighter. They waved in a moving band across the sky, a band that increased in intensity, faded, strengthened again. The streamers paraded from east to west. New shafts continually speared upward while the western sky grew rosy with a deepening reddish glow. Once a falling star drew its fine line of illumination across the northern lights. For nearly an hour the auroral display continued. At last the rosy hue in the west began to pale. Then, as we watched, the streamers, like the lessening flames of a dying fire, sank lower, grew dimmer, gradually faded from the sky.

Other auroras, seen from the Starfield, our north pasture, in subsequent years, remain vivid in recollection. In one we had the impression the shimmering light was descending like fine curtains of rain around us. In another, lightning came and went far off in the northwestern sky. In a third, over and over there drifted down to us the small frail voices of unseen songbirds migrating south across the vastness of a sky pulsing with the silvery shimmer of the polar lights.

Each of these storms is triggered by an explosion on the sun. In the far north, where lines of magnetic force come together, such displays at times are almost continual. Thus, the aurora provides a substitute sun that makes less dark the long night of the Arctic winter. In rhythm with the eleven-year cycle of sunspots, auroras increase and decrease in frequency. During the mid-1960s, we were in a period of relative inactivity, "the years of the quiet sun." Then in 1969 the excitement of auroral displays returned. On the twenty-third of March that year the most spectacular aurora of our lives began about 8:30 in the evening.

Bundled up in the thirty-degree temperature, we watched it from the Starfield. Around us patches of snow in the hollows of the meadow were flushed with a faint reddish tinge reflected from the glow in the sky. The air was still, the night silent. The play of auroral light absorbed us completely. We lived in our sense of sight.

Sometimes silver, sometimes frosty green, drifting or shooting upward, the sheets of shimmering light ascended toward the zenith. In sudden rushes they spread to right or left as though gusts of wind were driving powdery luminous snow before them. Everywhere the play of light was shifting, glowing, waxing, and waning. The whole sky seemed alive. We had the sensation of continually catching fleeting movements from the corners of our eyes.

In the north and east and west radiant patches, at first rose red, expanded and deepened in color. At times they were bordered by light almost electric blue. An airliner, high above us, flew through

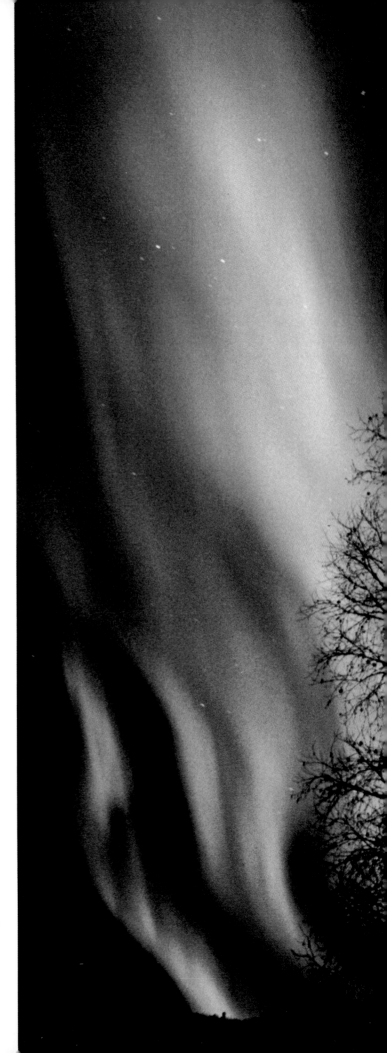

one reddish patch, its own red lights winking on and off. Toward the west, close beside one of the largest areas of red, a pale crescent moon gleamed faintly. To the north, over the ragged ebony line of the woods, the Big Dipper imperceptibly wheeled on its course through streamers and curtains of silvery light. Once, recalling our first aurora, a falling star drew an almost horizontal line through veils of white and patches of red. Here and there, where the glowing areas and the rising and falling curtains of light grew thin, stars shone brightly as though through windows.

And all around the horizon, shafts of white, at times suggesting the beams of searchlights, soared upward, frequently seeming, at the top of the sky, to overlap like the poles of a tepee—a vast celestial tepee with all the dimly visible earth enclosed beneath. In the stillness of the night, we had the impression of standing beneath a luminous insubstantial tent, a shimmering canopy of light. Never before nor since have we witnessed an auroral display of such magnitude—extending completely around the horizon.

For nearly two hours we watched while the movement and color continued. So stirring was the experience that we felt lifted from earth. The beauty of an aurora is all spirit. Even long after, the recollection of it brings back the emotion of magical moments. No other contact with the heavens at night that the Starfield has afforded has been so ethereal, so moving as those times when the shifting light of an aurora has filled the sky.

—*Edwin Way Teale, 1974*

——— ❅ ———

In the far north, where the aurora borealis is an almost nightly occurrence, Eskimo and Indian tribes of the area wove explanations of the light show into their legends and religious beliefs. Some Eskimos, for example, believed that the lights were caused by lanterns carried by spirits guiding lost souls to the afterworld.

Legend Of The Big Dipper

Two centuries ago, the Kiowas made a legend. My grandmother said:

Eight children were there at play, seven sisters and their brother. Suddenly the boy was struck dumb; he trembled and began to run upon his hands and feet. His fingers became claws, and his body was covered with fur. Directly there was a bear where the boy had been. The sisters were terrified; they ran, and the bear after them. They came to the stump of a great tree, and the tree spoke to them. It bade them climb upon it, and as they did so it began to rise into the air. The bear came to kill them, but they were just beyond its reach. It reared against the tree and scored the bark all around with its claws. The seven sisters were borne into the sky, and they became the stars of the Big Dipper.

From that moment, and so long as the legend lives, the Kiowas have kinsmen in the night sky.

Adapted from *The Way to Rainy Mountain*, by N. Scott Momaday.

Special Events

❊ *Geminid meteor shower:* Some 60 meteors an hour may be seen from December 7 to December 15. The star shower begins around midnight and ends in early morning.

❊ *Ursid meteor shower:* Somewhat less spectacular than the Geminid shower. These shooting stars can be seen from about December 14 to December 22.

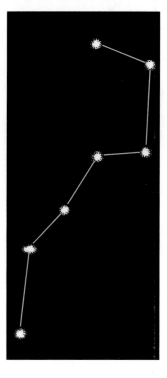

Casting eerie streamers across the night sky, an aurora borealis envelops the earth in other-worldly light, by Malcolm Lockwood.

DECEMBER 7

"Brer Fox and Canadas,"
acrylic painting by Chris
Walden, 1982.

MY FOX

In new snow, the tracks go blithely across the yard in the lee of the hedges, pausing here to investigate a tuft of grass, there to sniff at a small pile of brush. The tracks are like those of a small dog, but narrower and haired, and showing the marks of sharp claws. There may be fewer rabbits on the premises this winter but they will be more alert, for if we do not have a new resident fox, at least we are booked for occasional appearances.

Although a red fox may travel as much as twenty miles when hunted hard, which is considerably farther than most hunters will push him these days, he's a home-loving soul and normally ranges only a couple of miles from his den. But we have come to the dead of winter, when tender emotions begin to stir in the hearts of foxes. My transient may be only prospecting and, with four-legged vixens scarce in the neighborhood, may not come this way again.

The red fox, by and large, has been notably successful coexisting with man. Although his numbers have been fairly stable for the last couple of decades, they once swung in great extremes, probably following the cyclic irruptions of rabbits. For foxes depend on rabbits almost as squirrels depend on nuts, and, for Reynard, only an extraordinary fecundity among mice would make up for a dearth of cottontails.

Those who seek simple answers for complicated problems of ecology would make the fox the villain in game-bird and song-bird depletions, as once they blamed him for deviltry in the hen house. Occasionally a fox may develop such perilous tastes, and is likely to pay the penalty; but for foxes in general, mammals make up ninety percent of the menu, with mice making up half

A red fox eyes his world (right), by Erwin and Peggy Bauer. Below, a fox noses through the snow for a meal, by Stephen J. Krasemann.

the total in season, and rabbits half of it the year round. My fox, for instance, will eat more grapes than pheasants, and more apples than either.

This vain little gamin is a successful competitor, and thus, despite his usefulness and his splendor, men keep dogs to hunt him. And few will understand why, if that track doesn't come across my field again, I will stand diminished.

—*Dion Henderson, 1979*

CALL OF THE FOX

All sounds are sharper in winter; the air transmits better. At night I hear more distinctly the steady roar of the North Mountain. In summer it is a sort of complacent purr, as the breezes stroke down its sides; but in winter always the same low, sullen growl.

A severe artist! No longer the canvas and the pigments, but the marble and the chisel. When the nights are calm and the moon full, I go out to gaze upon the wonderful purity of the moonlight and the snow. The air is full of latent fire, and the cold warms me—after a different fashion from that of the kitchen stove. The world lies about me in a "trance of snow." The clouds are pearly and iridescent, and seem the farthest possible remove from the condition of a storm,—the ghosts of clouds, the indwelling beauty freed from all dross. I see the hills, bulging with great drifts, lift themselves up cold and white against the sky, the black lines of fences here and there obliterated by the depth of the snow. Presently a fox barks away up next the mountain, and I imagine I can almost see him sitting there, in his furs, upon the illuminated surface, and looking down in my direction. As I listen, one answers him from behind the woods in the valley. What a

42

. . . I imagine I can almost see him sitting there, in his furs, upon the illuminated surface, and looking down in my direction.

— ❄ —

wild winter sound,—wild and weird, up among the ghostly hills. Since the wolf has ceased to howl upon these mountains, and the panther to scream, there is nothing to be compared with it. So wild! I get up in the middle of the night to hear it. It is refreshing to the ear, and one delights to know that such wild creatures are among us. At this season Nature makes the most of every throb of life that can withstand her severity. How heartily she indorses this fox!

—John Burroughs, 1876

The small rodents which make up most of a fox's winter diet must build ventilation shafts to release poisonous carbon monoxide from their burrows under the snow. Along with the poisonous gas, the warm scent of the burrow's inhabitants wafts to the surface—and to foxes working the snowy meadows in search of a warm meal. But even when there are no shafts around, the fox is well-equipped for winter hunting. Its sensitive ears enable it to hear faint squeals and scratches through up to twelve inches of snow. Once the squeak is picked up, the fox leaps into the air, landing with nose and forepaws together. The impact breaks the snow's crust and, more likely than not, the fox gets its dinner.

— ❄ —

He was beautifully made: long, slender legs,
slender body, elegant brush.

RED FOX RIVIERA

One recent winter there was a dramatic snowstorm that brought a lot of people a lot of trouble, but we were lucky enough to have plenty of food and fuel and the storm caused us no problems. In fact, we enjoyed it. What follows is a report written just after the storm.

I found that the snow around the house was of a tricky and difficult depth. If I could ski, it would have been perfect. But since I can't I had to be content with a less glamorous sport called floundering. I started floundering out to the stable, breaking through the thin crust. I rounded a corner and surprised a fox snoozing on the ma-nure pile. This, I realized, must be the warmest spot in town. Its internal heat, plus its steep slope and the sun on its dark surface, had melted the snow, creating a sort of Red Fox Riviera. It seems foxes have known about alternate energy sources all along. Reluctantly, the fox got up, shook himself, and trotted off lightly on the delicate crust of the snow. No floundering for him. His coat was a lovely shade of orange. He was beautifully made: long, slender legs, slender body, elegant brush. He paused behind a bush to stare at me and then moved on.

—*Faith McNulty, 1980*

A fox's winter day: basking in the warm sun (left), by Wayne Lankinen; speeding home across the snow (above), by Hugh Morton.

DECEMBER 8

SNOW MEADOW

Thus come and go the bright sun-days of autumn, not a cloud in the sky, week after week until near December. Then comes a sudden change. Clouds of a peculiar aspect with a slow, crawling gait gather and grow in the azure, throwing out satiny fringes, and becoming gradually darker until every lake-like rift and opening is closed and the whole bent firmament is obscured in equal structureless gloom. Then comes the snow, for the clouds are ripe, the meadows of the sky are in bloom, and shed their radiant blossoms like an orchard in the spring. Lightly, lightly they lodge in the brown grasses and in the tasseled needles of the pines, falling hour after hour, day after day, silently, lovingly,—all the winds hushed,—glancing and circling hither, thither, glinting against one another, rays interlocking in flakes as large as daisies; and then the dry grasses, and the trees, and the stones are all equally abloom again. Thunder-showers occur here during the summer months, and impressive it is to watch the coming of the big transparent drops, each a small world in itself,—one unbroken ocean without islands hurling free through the air like planets through space. But still more impressive to me is the coming of the snow-flowers,—falling stars, winter daisies,—giving bloom to all the ground alike. Raindrops blossom brilliantly in the rainbow, and change to flowers in the sod, but snow comes in full flower direct from the dark, frozen sky.

The later snow-storms are oftentimes accompanied by winds that break up the crystals, when the temperature is low, into single petals and irregular dusty fragments; but there is comparatively little drifting on the meadow, so securely is it embosomed in the woods. From December to May, storm succeeds storm, until the snow is about fifteen or twenty feet deep, but the surface is always as smooth as the breast of a bird.

—*John Muir, 1894*

A snowy view of Yosemite Falls, by Frank S. Balthis.

THE SNOW

It sifts from Leaden Sieves—
It powders all the Wood.
It fills with Alabaster Wool
The Wrinkles of the Road—

It makes an Even Face
Of Mountain, and of Plain—
Unbroken Forehead from the East
Unto the East again—

It reaches to the Fence—
It wraps it Rail by Rail
Till it is lost in Fleeces—
It deals Celestial Vail

To Stump, and Stack—and Stem—
A Summer's empty Room—
Acres of Joints, where Harvests were,
Recordless, but for them—

It Ruffles Wrists of Posts
As Ankles of a Queen—
Then stills its Artisans—like ghosts—
Denying they have been—

      —Emily Dickinson, 1891

*A first snow caps a yellow
apple, by Robert P. Carr.*

. . . we stood dumbfounded as we came to a trail that led from yesterday's autumn into today's winter.

— ❁ —

A WINTER MUSKRAT

The first snow of the season began at dusk. It fell all night in wet, sticky flakes that clung where they landed. Peg and I took a walk in the morning through the silent wonderland. We marveled at the cottony puffs that rested on the remaining yellow leaves of the poplars. We exclaimed over the forks of the limbs, so brimful of snow that we couldn't tell where the branches joined. And we stood dumbfounded as we came to a trail that led from yesterday's autumn into today's winter.

The trail was a trail of blood.

We bent for a moment, scrutinizing the double line of webbed footprints, the thin drag mark of a tail. A muskrat, and a small one, from the looks. It had come up from the river bank and had made its way across the snowy lawn toward the corner of the house.

We followed the path with our eyes. It ended beneath the syringa bush. And there was the muskrat. He had gone as far as his strength would allow. Now he huddled beneath the bush, his face bitten and his nose almost gone.

We tried to piece the story together. The gravelly bank of our river supports a rather sparse vegetation along its steep sides: sedges, a few shrubs, a handful of struggling cattails. These have barely maintained a muskrat family for years, with little forage left over for grown youngsters. Ordinarily the young go poking along the shore in August and September to find their own patch of edible plants, but this little fellow had been different. He had probably refused to leave at the appointed time.

His parents may have grudgingly accepted his presence through those warm autumn days. But when four inches of snow covered nearly everything edible along that scanty riverbank, the picture changed. With raw survival at stake, the old muskrats turned on the youngster. One must perish or all would perish. And the end result of the family squabble was a brown furry object, the size of a small cat, huddled in misery beneath the syringa bush.

We threw an old coat over the wounded animal, then carefully unfolded it to where we could look at him. His nose would never be the same, but he'd survive. We put him in a large cage with a dishpan of water so he could keep his skin wet, and fed him apples and vegetables for a few days. That weekend we released him in a nearby swamp where the competition wasn't so keen.

—Ronald Rood, 1973

A curious muskrat surveys the wintry scene near its lodge, by Jack Couffer.

SNOW-FLAKES

Out of the bosom of the Air,
Out of the cloud-folds of her garments shaken,
Over the woodlands brown and bare,
Over the harvest-fields forsaken,
Silent, and soft, and slow
Descends the snow.

—Henry Wadsworth Longfellow, 1863

A gentle snow dusts a pair of
mallards, by Jan L. Wassink.

A BLANKET OF SNOW

Never was stuff so malleable as snow, so easy and quick to work, and never was artist so free as the wind. Now over the last year's nest is cocked a peaked new roof, now every fence post is capped, and the baldest ditch is softened to a slope like the flank of some great crouching beast. The very currents of the wind, that helped to shape the flake, are written, with the tracks of wild life, on the fields of white. Tomorrow, if the wind blows all night long, and more snow falls, the careless sculptor will have shaped the world all over again.

Snow, in this soft blanket form, is a kindly thing. Cold as it is, it forms a shelter for little creatures crouching in its lee.

—*Donald C. and Noel Peattie, 1950*

A cottontail snuggles in its snow-insulated burrow, by Robert Pollock.

If you have ever thought of snow as a white blanket stretching across the landscape, you have been right. For the small creatures that live beneath the snow—lemmings, voles, mice—the white cover is an essential shield against winter's cold. When snow accumulates two or three feet, ground temperature remains at about twenty degrees Fahrenheit, even when the temperature above the snow plummets to sixty degrees below zero.

—❄—

52

❄ Snow is not really white. Snow crystals are transparent, and as they lie by the millions on the ground, they reflect light in all directions, creating the white color of snow.

❄ Pink snow regularly blankets alpine areas of some western mountains, from the Sierra Nevadas in California to the Brooks Range in Alaska. The color comes from snow-dwelling algae that tint the white stuff in varying hues of pink and red. Some of these algae color the snow a watermelon red, and even perfume it with a watermelon aroma.

❄ Large snowflakes—about the diameter of a silver dollar—descend at about three-and-a-half miles an hour—roughly six times slower than a raindrop.

❄ A leading expert on snow estimates that it takes more than one million snow crystals to cover a two-square-foot area with ten inches of snow.

❄ Snow has probably fascinated mankind ever since the first human encountered a snowflake. The stuff of myths and fairy tales, snow has also been the subject of intense study.

The first recorded drawings of snowflakes were done by the Swedish archbishop and historian Olaus Magnus in 1555. Less than a century later, the German astronomer Johannes Kepler published "A New Year's Gift," a small treatise on the six-sided symmetry of snowflakes. At roughly the same time, René Descartes, the French philosopher and mathematician, published the first scientifically accurate sketches of flakes.

But the thrill of photographing snowflakes for the first time was left to an American farmer-turned-photographer—Wilson "Snowflake" Bentley of Jericho, Vermont. At the age of fourteen, Bentley saw his first snowflake through a cheap microscope—and his fascination began. Six years later, in January, 1855, he successfully photographed his first snowflake. Every winter for the next forty years, Bentley photographed snowflakes, leaving us a legacy of almost 5,000 snow portraits.

❄ The types of crystals that form help determine the kind of snow that covers the ground. In low-temperature clouds that hold little moisture, small granular crystals develop. These crystals fall to earth as fine powdery snow that easily drifts—the kind of snow that makes skis glide smoothly. In warmer clouds with a higher moisture content, six-sided crystals are more likely to

Snowflake photographs, by Wilson A. Bentley

form. As they fall, these crystals join together into large snowflakes that descend gently and slowly. This is the kind of snow that puts a heavy frosting on trees and houses, creating a winter wonderland.

❄ For most of us, snow is simply snow. But the people of the Far North, who for generations have had to plot their days in a world of almost constant snow, distinctions are critical. The Eskimos of Alaska's Kobuk Valley, for example, distinguish more than twelve kinds of snow. Where we require a whole phrase to describe each kind, the Eskimos use only one word. The following eight examples represent only a portion of their rich snow terminology:

Anniu – Snow
Qali – Snow that collects on trees
Api – Snow on the ground
Upsik – Wind-beaten snow
Siqoq – Smoky snow or drifting snow
Siqoqtoaq – Snow melted by the sun and refrozen into a crust
Kimoaqruk – Drift
Qamaniq – Bowl shaped depression in snow around base of trees

DECEMBER 9

"Wolf Pack in Moonlight,"
acrylic painting by Robert
Bateman, 1977.

TIMBER WOLVES

I could hear them plainly now on both sides of the river, could hear the brush crack as they hurdled windfalls in their path. Once I thought I saw one, a drifting gray shadow against the snow, but it was only a branch swaying in the light of the moon. When I heard the full-throated bawling howl, I should have had chills racing up and down my spine. Instead, I was thrilled to know that the big grays might have picked up my trail and were following me down the glistening frozen highway of the river.

It was a beautiful night for travel—twenty below, and the only sound the steady swish and creak of my snowshoes on the crust. There was a great satisfaction in knowing that the wolves were in the country, that it was wild enough and still big enough for them to roam and hunt. That night the wilderness of the Quetico-Superior was what the voyageurs had known two hundred years before, as primitive and unchanged as before discovery.

The river ahead narrowed to where two points of timber came out from either bank, and as I approached, I sensed instinctively the possibilities of attack. I was familiar with the wolf lore of the Old World, the packs on the steppes of Russia, the invasion of farms and villages, and had I believed the lurid tales of our early settlers and explorers, I might have been afraid. To the best of my knowledge, however, for the past twenty-five years there has never been a single authenticated instance of unprovoked attack on man.

But still there was a feeling of uneasiness, and I knew that if the animals were concerned with anything but satisfying their curiosity, the narrows would be the place for a kill. A swift rush from both points at the same time, a short, unequal scuffle in the snow, and it would be all over. My bones would go down with the ice in the spring, and no one would ever hear the story and no one would be able to explain.

As I neared the points of spruce, I could almost hear the crash of heavy bodies against windfalls and brush. Weighing a hundred, even as much as a hundred and twelve pounds or more, timber wolves are huge and powerful, can bring down a caribou or a moose, have nothing to fear on the entire continent but man. I knew that I was being watched, a lone dark spot moving slowly along the frozen river.

Then, far ahead, way beyond the dangerous points, two shadows broke from cover and headed directly down the river toward me. I stopped, slipped off my pack, and waited. Nearer and nearer they came, running with the easy, loose-jointed grace that only the big timber wolves seem to have. A hundred yards away they stopped and tried to get my wind; they wove back and forth, swaying as they ran. Then, about fifty feet away they stopped and looked me over. In the moonlight their gray hides glistened and I could see the greenish glint of their eyes. Not a movement or a sound. We stood watching each other as though such meetings were expected and commonplace.

As suddenly as they had appeared, they whirled and were off down the river, two drifting forms against the ice. Never before had I been that close, possibly never again would I see the glint in timber wolves' eyes or have such a chance to study their free and fluid movement. Once more came the long howl, this time far from the river, and then I heard them no more.

A little later I pushed open the door of the little cabin and touched a match to the waiting tinder in the stove. As I sat there listening to the roar of it and stowing away my gear, I realized fully what I had seen and what I had felt. Had it not been twenty below, I would have left the door opened wide so as not to lose the spell of the moonlit river and the pack ranging its shores.

After I was warmed and had eaten my supper, I stepped outside once more. The river was still aglisten, and the far shore looked black and somber. An owl hooted back in the spruce, and I knew what that meant in the moonlit glades. A tree cracked sharply with the frost, and then it was still, so still that I could hear the beating of my heart. At last I caught what I was listening for—the long-drawn quavering howl from over the hills, a sound as wild and indigenous to the north as the muskegs or the northern lights. That was wilderness music, something as free and untamed as there is on this earth.

—Sigurd F. Olson, 1957

— ❁ —

Wolves have compact, narrow paws that easily sink in deep snow. Thus, wolves are more likely to live in areas with little snow or where the snow is frequently crusted. The hard crust will support the weight of a wolf, but not that of some of the wolf's prey, giving the wolf an advantage when hunting elk, moose, and caribou.

— ❁ —

BUILT-IN SNOWSHOES

The Snowshoe-rabbit, the Wabasso of Hiawatha, is a wonderful creature, the product of a snowdrift crossed with a little Brown Hare. The terror of the northern woods is—not cold, there are many ways of meeting that—but deep snow. Snow is the fearful menace, snow that covers up the food supplies, that robs the swiftest of its speed, and leaves it at the mercy of the foes that are winged or otherwise equipped to follow fast and lay it low.

Nature has tried many means of saving her own from the snow-death, one is—sleeping till it is over; this is the way of the Woodchuck. An-

other is storing up food and hiding; this is the manner of the Wood-mouse. Yet another is stilts; the plan that the Moose has adopted. The last is snowshoes. This is the simplest, most scientific, and best—and the plan of the Snowshoe-hare.

The Moose is like the wading bird of the shore, that has stilts and can wade well for a space, yet soon reaches the limit, where it is no better off than a land bird. But the Snowshoe is like the swimmer, it skims over the surface where it will, not caring if there be 1 or 1000 feet of the element below it. In this lies Wabasso's strength.

—Ernest Thompson Seton, 1909

— ❄ —

The snowshoe hare's specialized feet give it a double advantage. Besides enabling the hare to move efficiently through deep snows, the built-in snowshoes enable the animal to "float" atop the snow and to reach ever higher evergreen meals with each snowfall.

Marching single file, a herd of mule deer plows a deep furrow in a Wyoming snowdrift, by Erwin A. Bauer.

DASHING THROUGH THE SNOW

Wildlife Solutions

❋ Caribou, the preeminent long-distance travelers over wintry terrain, count on remarkable foot adaptations for their treks over the snow. When the snows blanket its world, the caribou's hoof is no longer worn down by the hard tundra soil. The outer edge of the hoof grows out, forming a sharp-edged scoop—an ideal traction blade for traversing icy terrain. Special oily bristles also grow around the hooves in winter, preventing loose snow from sticking to the foot and weighing it down.

❋ Like the snowshoe hare, the arctic fox and the lynx grow an extra pad of hair on their feet. The extra hair functions like a snowshoe and helps keep the feet warm in winter.

❋ Moose and caribou rely on their stiltlike legs to clear deep snow. Where humans may easily tire in a snow depth of eight inches, caribou, for example, can easily walk for miles in snow sixteen inches deep. Moose legs also have special joints that let the animals swing their legs sideways—an extra insurance for not getting mired in deep drifts.

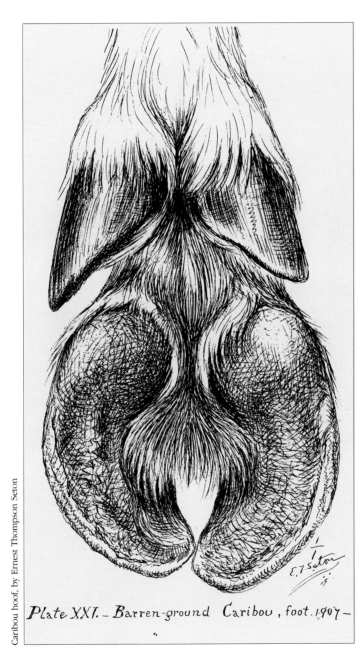

Caribou hoof, by Ernest Thompson Seton

Plate XXI. — Barren-ground Caribou, foot. 1907 —

❋ Having no special adaptations for moving through deep snow, deer and elk rely on a follow-the-leader strategy. The lead animal breaks trail and compacts the snow; the rest of the herd follow, single file, along the leader's deep furrow.

❋ Weasels usually move through snow by long bounds. If the snow gets too deep, or if a weasel encounters an especially deep drift, the creature dives in, swims through the snow, and emerges some distance away.

❋ For the bison, moving in deep snow is a matter of brute strength. The short-legged, powerful creature breaks trail like a living bulldozer: It swings its massive head from side to side, plowing through snow drifts as deep as four feet.

Human Solutions

❋ Eskimos living in the Arctic tundra, where snow is generally hard and dense, developed a sled, "komatik," especially designed for this terrain. The sled rides on a pair of runners, and even when heavily loaded it can be pulled easily across the wind-hardened snow.

❋ For the Indians living in areas of deep and fluffy snow, the problem was how not to sink. They developed the toboggan, a sled with a flat, runnerless underside that could be dragged over the light snow without sinking. These Indians also developed two kinds of snowshoes: one, large with fine webbing, for walking on soft snow; the other, smaller with wider webbing, for walking in denser snow.

DECEMBER 10

WINTER IN THE SOUTHWEST

The southwestern winter is full of contrasts—warm deserts and high, cold forests; arid mesas and sparkling lakes and streams. Wildlife here, however, offers less seasonal contrast than any other part of the country.

A Christmas walk will find all the familiar wildlife neighbors—deer, jackrabbits, doves, quail, ground squirrels, 'coons and skunks—right at home, for their summer and winter homes are at the same address. We'll find northern waterfowl of all kinds settling down in their winter places for variety, but otherwise the habitats show more contrast than the winter wildlife.

A Christmas walk can go through as many as seven different life zones in a few miles. In the lower elevations and desert, we can find both human and wild residents enjoying the moderate daytime temperatures—even welcoming the occasional dusting of snow that frosts the sunburned rocks.

But if we move a thousand feet higher, we find the desert giving way to low mountains, with bighorn sheep, coyotes, cougars, and such exotics as the ring-tail cat and comical coatimundi. Higher, at the 5,000-foot level, we'll see snow, with antelope, bears, turkeys, band-tail pigeons, and trout. Still higher, we'll find ponderosa pines standing in deep snow—and elk!

So to the Southwesterner, the question of a Christmas hike may not be "shall we?", but "where?". This striking cross-section of topography, climate, plant life and wildlife guarantees something to please the eye of any nature lover. The coolness, the silence, the color and life of the Southwest will reward our Christmas hike wherever we go.

—Bob Schimmel, 1968

A view of the snowy Huachuca Mountains in southeastern Arizona, by Steven C. Wilson.

61

Not once had I seen an animal, yet I had experienced ... a tense natural drama, narrated by tracks in the snow.

— ❋ —

STORIES IN THE SNOW

I was deep in the Yellowstone backcountry, gliding along on cross-country skis on a sparkling winter day, when I noticed a fresh trail in the snow. The tightly clustered tracks told of a mule deer in flight, moving in great bounds toward a nearby slope. I altered my course to follow the trail and soon saw some coyote tracks, which poured in from one side and then the other, overtaking and obscuring the hoof marks. Though I knew that coyotes only occasionally stalk deer, the jumbled paw prints indicated that a pair of the predators were apparently in pursuit of the larger animal. I kicked hard against the skis, pushing ahead faster, reading the snow on the run.

The trail led up a low bench and over a ridge. Straining, I huffed to the top, expecting at any moment to see a confrontation between the animals. Instead, the tracks swerved on the spine of the ridge and headed toward some timber. Then, suddenly, the coyote tracks veered off, slowed and meandered. The hoof marks, meanwhile, continued straight ahead and disappeared into the thick pine and fir. The chase was over. Not once had I seen an animal, yet I had experienced what I assumed was a tense natural drama, narrated by tracks in the snow. Wildlife signs are not always so dramatic, of course, but all animals leave a variety of markings in their habitat that tell something about their lives.

There are dozens of other signs that mark an animal's presence. A felled tree may signify that a beaver has been at work; several rows of holes in a tree trunk probably display the efforts of a member of the woodpecker family. In winter, a leafy area or bare ground, surrounded by snow, may indicate where a deer has spent the night. Taken together, such signs form a portrait of life in the wild for anyone who takes the time to look carefully. And quite often, the tracking game can unfold a unique story all its own.

One November morning in northern Michigan, I found some red fox prints in new snow. The tracks ran along the edge of a woodland meadow, veering now and then, and circling the dense clumps of brush. The reason became obvious when I noticed the spindly, lightly tufted tracks of a ruffed grouse, leading into one such tangle. Apparently, the fox had stopped at some patches of vegetation to sniff out a potential meal. However, the snow did not show any signs of a struggle.

Soon the tracks turned away from the edge of the forest and cut into the meadow. There, the

A coyote treks across a snow-covered streambed, by Tom and Pat Leeson.

signs showed that the fox had moved through the high grass and pawed in the snow. Perhaps the animal was looking for field mice.

Eventually, the trail cut through the open center of the meadow and stopped near the base of a large rock. Paw scratches indicated where the fox had probed the snow-covered opening of an old den. I brushed away more snow and studied the foot-wide entrance hole, finding a weather-bleached bone from an earlier meal.

The tracks led out of the meadow and into a second-growth stand of jack pine and birch. The prints began to appear in bunches as the animal trotted ahead. The tracks indicated that the fox had jumped over a fallen birch and then darted under a sapling pine. A small amount of blood and fur marked the spot, but there were no signs of a struggle in the area. I puzzled over this until I noticed a small trench excavated in the snow.

During lean months, foxes eat as much as they can of a kill and bury the rest for a future meal. Having had no luck that morning with grouse or mice, this fox must have returned to its cache.

From experience, I knew that after eating, the fox would probably return to the sunny meadow, curl into a tight ball and doze away the day. At that point, I felt that if I continued to follow the creature, I would probably flush it from its nap and cause it to burn up needed calories. So I decided to move on. It wasn't necessary that I see the fox itself. After all, I had enjoyed a pleasurable morning just by following the wily predator's tracks.

—*Anthony Acerrano, 1982*

A snowy winter landscape is ideal for reading wildlife's tracks, by Arnout Hyde, Jr.

READING ANIMAL SIGNATURES

❊ Tracks in the snow reveal the presence and secret habits of many animals that would escape our notice in other seasons. And the beauty of the sport of tracking is that you can pursue it in cities and suburbs as well as in the deep wilderness. Here are some tips to help you read stories written in the snow.

❊ The best snow for finding tracks is neither too dry nor too wet. Dry, powdery snow can easily drift, erasing prints. Wet snow can melt around prints, obscuring them.

❊ The best time to find tracks is the morning, since most mammals are active at night. Animals normally don't go abroad during a storm or for a few hours after it, however; so if a snowstorm ends during the night or early morning, you'll probably have to wait until the following morning to see tracks.

❊ The best place to find tracks is where two habitats meet: between a forest and a field, or the bank of a stream or pond.

❊ If you're baffled by a track, check above you. Snow falling or melting from roof eaves, trees, or power lines can create "mystery tracks," as well as obscure real tracks.

The following tracks are the four basic patterns left by common North American mammals. Tracks should be read from left to right.

1. Tracks in a nearly straight line: Members of the dog, cat, and deer families (foxes, coyotes, bobcats, lynx, deer, moose) make tracks of this kind when they walk or trot.

2. Tracks in evenly spaced pairs or bunches: Members of the weasel family (weasels, otters, mink, fishers), with the exception of the slow-moving skunk, make tracks of this kind when they bound.

3. Tracks in which the hind feet land beside or in front of the front feet: This is the gallop pattern of rabbits, hares, squirrels, and mice. As the creature speeds up (track farthest to right) the space between the front and hind feet becomes greater.

4. Tracks in two alternating rows: These tracks are typical of waddling, heavy-bodied animals such as raccoons, muskrats, opossums, porcupines, and beavers.

The tracks of birds walking or hopping can be mistaken for mouse or vole tracks. To tell them apart, look for the tracks to end abruptly and for wing marks in the snow where the bird took off.

Adapted from *A Guide to Nature in Winter*, by Donald W. Stokes.

DECEMBER 11

ADIRONDACK SPRUCE

Up in the Adirondacks winter's coming is marked by more than the bladed wind across the lakes and the snow flurries against the grey skies. On the hillsides and across distant lake shores the tall evergreens, particularly the spruce, are slowly darkening. Close up, the spruce are a heavy lifeless green but at a distance they are almost black with the live color drained from them. That blackness marks the winter woods as much as the bare grasping branches of the maples or the trim green of the hemlock.

The old spruce, high on the side of Marcy and McIntyre, have already been snow-tipped. Yet at the end of each branch, even the smallest, are the little brown buds set ready for next year's growth. On the spruce is the promise of new life that will come to the woods on some far-off day. A man may need to look close to see those buds but they are there and with them the promise that the winter will not last forever.

—*William Chapman White, 1960*

— ❄ —

Evergreen trees are ideally suited to winter. Their tough, green needles stay on all winter, continuing to produce food even in the harshest cold spells. The needle's waxy coating sheds snow easily, and the steeple shape of most conifers encourages the heavy snow to slide to the ground, rather than weight the tree to the breaking point.

The gentle contours of snow-covered hills provide a backdrop for hardy evergreens, by David Muench.

© Maynard Reece 1982

THE PINE WOODS

The chit-chat of the woods is sometimes hard to translate. Once in midwinter I found in the droppings under a grouse roost some half-digested structures that I could not identify. They resembled miniature corncobs about half an inch long. I examined samples of every local grouse food I could think of, but without finding any clue to the origin of the 'cobs.' Finally I cut open the terminal bud of a jackpine, and in its core I found the answer. The grouse had eaten the buds, digested the pitch, rubbed off the scales in his gizzard, and left the cob, which was, in effect, the forthcoming candle. One might say that this grouse had been speculating in jackpine 'futures.'

—*Aldo Leopold, 1949*

— ❄ —

In winter, when snows blanket their dinner table, grouse must resort to feeding from buds, needles, catkins, and berries in trees and bushes. To be able to climb the ice-encrusted trunks and branches, some species of grouse grow a set of winter crampons—a horny comb on each foot. When spring comes the crampons fall off.

"Heavy Snow—Ruffed Grouse," oil painting by Maynard Reece, 1982.

In the Colorado Rockies, an aspen's branches cradle a light load of snow, by Ed Cooper.

IN THE ASPEN GROVE

Westerners have a special feeling about aspen. It is the only tall deciduous grove-forming tree of the montane area. Alder, willow, dogwood, and mountain maple are all shrubs or shrublike trees and, on our land, are never over twelve to fourteen feet high. Conifers have a majestic monotony, like someone who is always right. They are too timeless to mark the seasons. But aspen has éclat, a glorious brashness in defiance of the rules, the flapper who does the Charleston in the midst of the grand waltz. The landscape would be dull indeed without them.

In the winter the aspen woodland is a thousand eyes. When the wind blows, the trees of the grove rock in unison, keening over lost summers. Empty black branches, formed like clutching hands, scratch at the sky. The boles are pallid in the white winter sunlight, gleaming like bleached bones, only a shade darker than the shadowed snow at their bases. At the foot of each trunk is a tiny crescent of open ground, facing the sun. The warmth reflected by the light-colored trunks warms the snow and opens the turf to foraging by the deer mice who live in the community.

A deer mouse hunts at night and his tracks through the aspen grove form cat's cradles from one tree to the next. The amount of tracking shows this to be a busy grove. Perhaps it is still warm enough in December to find bark beetles or a few late sluggardly insects. The seedhead of a black-eyed Susan lies shredded. And then the neat precise tracks lead to a sprig of wild timothy. Here the dried stem is bent down by two tiny forefeet—the seeds nibbled, and chaff spilled on the new snow. And then tiny paired footprints hop on, incessantly searching for food to keep body heat up in the below-zero nights to come.

—*Ann Zwinger, 1981*

❋ The quaking aspen is perhaps the most widely distributed North American tree. Stands of aspen are found from eastern Canada to Alaska, and south into alpine reaches of Mexico. Aspen groves also flourish on the slopes of the Rocky Mountains, the Cascades, and the Sierra Nevadas.

❋ Grouse, porcupine, deer, snowshoe hare, rabbits, and black bear are just a few of the many creatures that feed on or find shelter in aspen trees.

❋ Beavers are particularly fond of the tree's bark and branches. In winter, they stash aspen and other trees under the ice near their home and feed from the stockpile throughout the cold season.

❋ Ruffed grouse depend on aspen to such an extent that, within the bird's range, grouse populations and aspen stands usually appear together. In winter, the grouse prefer aspen buds over any other food; stands of young trees give the birds ideal cover.

❋ As pioneer trees colonizing disturbed land, aspen provide shelter so that other trees such as spruce, fir, and pine can grow. Furthermore, aspen stands protect the soil from freezing: More snow accumulates under the deciduous aspen than under the evergreen conifers, providing an insulating blanket for the land.

❋ Humans, too, have used aspen for centuries. The tree's winter buds, for example, have been processed into an antiseptic liquid for cuts and scrapes, a resinous tonic for the kidneys, and a salve to fight colds and flu. Mormon settlers found aspen wood perfect for building furniture and for crafting kitchen utensils. Aspen boards were often used for barn floors and horse stalls because the wood doesn't easily splinter.

DECEMBER 12

DANCING HARES

The hare trail wound north between the spruces, away from the feeding grounds in the aspen thicket. The snow was deep, and enabled the hares to reach new unforaged heights in the dense aspens. They were doing well in there, snipping off the twig ends with their efficient teeth. The neat, beveled prunings of hares are quite different from the ragged work of deer, who grind and tear the browse off with cud-chewing molars.

Snowshoe hares lie at the center of a wintering world, forming a central link in the chain of energies, which ecologists are always trying to piece together. Where there are white pines or birch or young browse of any sort there are hares, and where there are hares one is almost certain to come upon the twin-print hunting trail of a weasel, or the dotted-line track of a red fox. The hares lie in the middle of winter space as well as energy; they neither scrabble beneath the snow as their more southern cousins, the cottontails, do, nor do they climb above it. And the hares are equipped, superbly equipped, for winter.

The year that the snow was so deep and the aspen thicket such a popular spot for the hares' nocturnal foraging I discovered something strange about them. One often makes the mistake of thinking that all animals ever have time to do is to eat or hide or hunt. This may be true enough, at least of animals less well-equipped and in winters more severe, but it was not true of hares that year. The trail from their feeding grounds ended deep in the woods at an open circle of tall evergreens.

Camouflaged by its fluffy white coat, an arctic hare contemplates its snowy domain, by David R. Gray.

Five trails came together there, and where they met a circle a yard broad had been tramped into the snow by many hares all hopping on their hind feet. My immediate impression was that the hares had been dancing, and others who have seen such hare-circles have come to the same conclusion.

—*Diana Kappel-Smith, 1980*

— ❄ —

Nocturnal dancing seems to be only one type of odd behavior among hares. One of the snowshoe hare's northern cousins, the arctic hare of the northernmost arctic islands of Canada, hops on its hind feet like a kangaroo.

According to Canadian mammalogist, A. W. Frank Banfield, when one of these hares is alarmed, it will make a getaway, bounding "on its hind toes with its forelegs dangling loosely or pressed to its breast." Scientists don't know quite why these hares have adopted the two-legged hop, but Banfield thinks the flat openness of the arctic-island terrain may have something to do with it. Whatever the reason, he says, "It seems to be their passing gear."

Arctic hares, at three times the weight of snowshoe hares, are the largest in North America. They have strong claws on their forefeet with which they dig for food through crusted snow, and have even been known to eat meat. They dress in a fluffy white coat, and only their eyes and ear tips show up against the white expanse of their northern home. Indeed, a perfect camouflage—except, perhaps, when they do the kangaroo hop.

RESOURCEFUL RABBIT

During the December of 1886 I saw a chase that had a very unexpected end. I was out with a friend hunting in the sandhills north-east of Carberry. The Snowshoe-rabbits were very abundant in the thicker woods, and there were some in an open grove where we halted to feed our horses. While there I saw one running about at full speed, and after it what at first I took for a smaller Rabbit in hot pursuit. As it circled in full flight around our sleigh a number of times, I learned the cause of its haste. The smaller one behind was not a Rabbit at all, but a White Weasel, plunging along with tremendous energy through the snow, and evidently running this Rabbit down. The Weasel was winning. He was within a few yards of his victim, when at last, the Rabbit, in desperation took refuge near my feet, under the sleigh, and the Weasel, deciding to be discreet, ran off before I could lay hands on a gun. There is not the least doubt that the Rabbit feared me as an enemy, for shortly before it had been running from me. But it did as many others have done in dire extremity, and in this case at least proved it the part of wisdom, for a little later it went its way in peace.

—*Ernest Thompson Seton, 1909*

BRUISED EGO

It always delights me to come upon a story that does not end in tragedy, but in a bruised ego. It had been a bitterly cold, open winter until a few days before, when a light snow had fallen. Followed by a sudden thaw, the snow had melted. Then a heavy rain began to fall. Because the frozen earth could not absorb the deluge, water formed puddles, some several yards long, in every natural pocket. Abruptly, winter regained control and rammed the thermostat down to zero. The falling

Rabbits and hares lead lives of many dangers. Among their predators: long-tailed weasels (above), by Phil Dotson, and bobcats (left), by Leonard Lee Rue III. To escape from danger, some arctic hares hop away on two legs—kangaroo-fashion (opposite), by David R. Gray.

75

A lynx (below) stalks its winter food, by C. C. Lockwood. A snowshoe hare, the lynx's main prey, huddles motionless to escape detection (right), by Charlie Ott.

rain turned to snow. Soon, three inches of powder camouflaged ice-covered pools.

Shortly after entering the woods, I came across a cat track made several hours before. The cat was traveling at its usual hunting pace: walking silently . . . freezing . . . waiting . . . as it zigzagged through woods and swamps. Steady, one paw in front of the other, the tracks finally led down a slight ridge. At the edge of an alder swamp, they came to a sudden stop. The cat's pace changed to nine-foot bounds. One . . . two . . . three . . . a turn to the right . . . a long, splayed mark ending in disaster.

While stalking the ridge, this cat had spotted a hare hopping slowly along the edge of the swamp thirty yards below. The cat froze, waiting until its dinner was fifty feet away. Br'er Rabbit, suddenly realizing it was either quit eating or be eaten, shifted into high. In trying to intercept a fleeing dinner, the cat had to make an unplanned turn. The attack that had started from solid snow ended on ice. Tom's feet went out from under him as he slid, head over bobtail, for fifteen feet, to crash into some bushes. I could see where he got up, shook himself, let out a string of cat curses, and shaking a clenched paw toward the alder swamp, snarled, "Just wait 'til next time, Bunny Boy."

—John Kulish, 1969

THE LYNX AND THE HARE

When nature decided that the lynx should be chiefly dependent on the snowshoe hare for his welfare, she seems to have initiated a similar development for survival in both species. To simplify the unknown complications, we might say that the snowshoe rabbit had to develop snowshoes to escape the lynx, and the lynx had to develop the same type of footgear to catch the rabbit. The rabbit, already having strong hind legs, developed a snowshoe type of foot where it would do the most good—on the hind legs. The lynx developed the snowshoe effect on all feet; the forefeet, being a little larger to start with, remained larger. Consequently, relationships remained nip and tuck between them, and both species have prospered so far as their mutual relationships are concerned.

—Adolph Murie, 1961

— ❈ —

The lynx and the snowshoe hare are linked by much more than twin adaptations. So closely tied are the two species, that the ups and downs in lynx populations mirror similar fluctuations in the hare populations.

For about ten years, snowshoe hare populations steadily rise in numbers. By the end of the upswing, hares by the thousands hop through the boreal forests of North America and the lynx finds abundant food.

Then, probably due to disease caused by overcrowding and the fact that the available food supply is not enough for so many hares, the snowshoes undergo a massive die-off: Many young and some adults don't survive the winters; fewer hares are born each year. In three or four years, the forests are almost empty of hares. Lynx populations, finding their major food source nearly gone, also begin to decline. Until, that is, the snowshoes start their upward trend again.

DECEMBER 13

THE ANCIENTS

One need not go into history to find the reasons for veneration of the evergreen tree or bough as a part of the Christmas season. They are of the enduring things of this earth, and man has known them as long as man has been here. The pine, the spruce, the hemlock, the fir—all those conifers that know no leafless season—have been held in special favor when man would have symbols of life that outlast all winters. And even more enduring, in geologic time, are the ground pine, the ground cedar, and the club mosses, most venerable of all the evergreens.

We gather them now, even as the ancients gathered them reaching for the reassurance of enduring green life at the time of the winter solstice. For the pines and their whole family were old when the first man saw them. Millions of years old, even then, even at a time when millions of years had no meaning. When we gather them we are reaching back, back into the deep recesses of time. But, even as the ancients, we are reaching for reassurance, for the beauty of the living green but also for that green itself, the green of life that outlasts the gray winds, the white frosts, and the glittering snow of winter.

So we bring in the pine, the spruce, the hemlock—and now, because of the cultivation of Christmas trees on a wide scale, we can do so without desecrating the natural forest. We bring the festoons of ground pine and partridgeberry, feeling a kinship with enduring things. They help us to catch, if only briefly, that needed sense of hope and understandable eternity.

—*Hal Borland, 1979*

Ground pine pokes through the snow (left), by Gene Ahrens. Bedecked with holiday greens, a fireplace (right) brightens a New Jersey home, by H. Armstrong Roberts.

Season's greetings: A decorated Christmas tree glows within a New England home (above), by Clyde H. Smith; a wreath hangs from a Williamsburg, Virginia, door (right), by Nicholas Foster.

CHRISTMAS

We climbed the straight tamarack
In those days,
Clinging fast to limb and limb,
Inspecting branches for strong footholds,
Leaning out to reach the little cones,
To discover the best ones were
Really at the top
Where the wind pushed and pulled the spire point,
The red-winged blackbird's perch,
Now grown cold and vacant
In winter's air.
The needles dropped away
From the deciduous conifer
To leave the twigs all bare,
A brittle silhouette above the humps of swamp,
And little saucers of blue ice.
Our footprints to the tree
In the snow looked small and gray,
Frozen writings of mute reality,
Our sudden past. We would trace them
Home again, our pockets full of cones
For school children to paint
And weave with yarn into chains
To hang upon another tree.

—Claire Mattern, 1975

*Red and white poinsettia
plants and Norfolk Island pine
boughs bring holiday cheer, by
Gary Mottau.*

Green Wreath

Materials needed:
Masonite or cardboard; glue; assorted greens; green plastic wrap or strips of dry-cleaner bags; wire for hanger; ribbon; floral picks; berries or other trims.

Tools needed:
Saber saw for Masonite; strong scissors for cardboard; clippers.

Cut a circle of Masonite the size that suits your purpose best. Use a saber saw to cut out the inner circle. If a saber saw is not available, and the wreath will not be out in the weather, substitute cardboard for the base. Cut two pieces of cardboard and glue them together for strength. The most common size is twelve inches in diameter, with a three-inch center. The beauty of this wreath, aside from the ease with which it can be made, is that it can be cut into any size and shape desired.

Wrap the ring using green plastic wrap from the florist, or dry cleaner bags doubled and cut into strips. Don't overlap them. When one strip ends, tie another to it, as the knots will not show on the wreath.

Many kinds of greens may be used for one wreath—including clippings from shrubbery, since pieces need only be two or three inches long. The greens should be "hardened" before using, so the wreath will stay fresh. Harden greens by placing the stems in very warm water overnight.

After the ring is completely wound with plastic, tuck short pieces of greens into the plastic strips as if they were being tucked into a pocket. Do one row, then the next, working your way around the wreath. Be generous with the greens; if they're skimpy, the wreath will not hold together. Twist a wire around the top of the frame for a hanger, and trim with small ribbon bows attached to floral picks, or with a large ribbon bow. Tuck berries here and there among the greens.

A wreath may also be made by stuffing a purchased wire wreath form with damp sphagnum moss, wrapping it with florist's plastic wrap, and inserting the greens into the moss. Boxwood is generally used this way; it makes a heavy, long-lasting wreath.

A Decorated Six-Pointed Star

Materials needed:
Wood screen molding; nails; staples; fine wire on a spool; treated lycopodium; hot glue; everlastings or paper flowers.

Tools needed:
Saw; staple gun; hammer; glue gun.

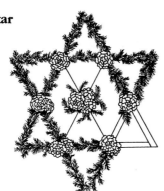

This wall design of a hexagonal star was found in an 1888 issue of *The Ladies' Home Journal.* It was constructed of thin strips of wood with the pieces nailed, wired, or stapled where they intersect. Wood called screen molding—or lattice strips, if you can find them—is a good size and weight—three-quarters of an inch wide and one-quarter of an inch thick.

Small pieces of evergreens may be lashed to these wooden pieces with fine-gauge spool wire; or if treated lycopodium is used, it may be stapled in place or held in place with hot glue from a glue gun. The glue gun works well with light-weight materials.

After the star is completely covered with greens, a cluster of flowers may be wired onto each intersection, for color. The flowers may be everlastings, such as strawflowers, or small paper flowers, so long as they have wire stems so that they may be attached to the star.

A little nosegay in the center adds to the whole design and may be attached by fine wires extending from the four intersections, as shown in the sketch.

Both crafts adapted from *The Gift of Christmas Past,* by Sunny O'Neil

---

Tips for preserving your decorations ever green
❋ Cut evergreens will keep best if stored at just-above-freezing temperature. Scrape the bark off cut ends or crush them with a hammer and put them in water.
❋ Holly and ivy need moisture, so stuff sphagnum moss (or florist's Oasis) around the cuttings.
❋ Keep all evergreen arrangements in the coolest possible place, and mist them often.

Adapted from *Blair & Ketchum's Country Journal,* December 1983

DECEMBER 14

THE WINTER MARSH

During the night, the marsh froze hard. For days, the sun had fought the freeze. It lit the cattail water gold and spun off six-sided diamonds of light from stalks of frost. Before the freeze, the marsh was a desperately tired place; summer wreckage everywhere, blackbird feathers forlorn in gray water, the bulrushes panzer-driven. The ice changed all that. It crept in, transparent and insecure at first, and muskrats smashed through it like tiny icebreakers. The ice persisted and the marsh was torn by a tumble of ducks reaching for black-water landings in thick early snow. The ice became blue and powerful; mergansers and goldeneyes lingered in narrowing pools until, one final frozen morning, the marsh was abandoned completely. Or so it seemed. Ice set the marsh in colored stone, held it still for the wild-watching eye, the silent artist, the motionless owl.

At first, the marsh's refrigerated death, its transfixion of all action, suggested a perfect wasteland. Nothing moved. But because there was time enough now to watch, and ample memory to stimulate, this was transparently a loose dictatorship. The ice had caught nothing unprepared. At night a rattle of dry stalks sounded, empty scabbards with the summer drawn out of them. In day, chickadees slid down the stalks and their feet encircled sleeping bees packed in vegetable corridors.

The marsh was made, it seemed, of pitiless colored stone, but this was a device to trick the transitory watcher. It moved, violent, strong, and willful. It moved and cattail jungles, still erect but

The rising sun lifts a veil of fog in a Yellowstone National Park marsh, by Jeff Gnass.

84

Ice set the marsh in colored stone, held it still for the wild-watching eye, the silent artist, the motionless owl.

— ❄ —

shorn from their roots, moved obediently with it. A mountain wind spent days trying out different forms of snow drifts, but gave up when its designs became too complex.

The marsh blended its shores—coasts of ice decorated with flowers of frost—into snow-drifted land. An ice window showed a distorted, familiar face, and a mink flickered away underwater. Shrews drilled ice tunnels, and moles, still digging with summer energy, dropped into the water and swam off. The silent blue ice revealed nothing of the torpedoing mammals and rudely awakened fish, the drowsy, jolted insects, the hunt continuing without rebate.

Precise crow footprints walked to a chiseled hole in the ice where an old dog muskrat, deep-frozen, was revisited daily. Weasels, whiter than snow, leaped into mice-riddled drifts; desperate tenants screamed injustice. Horned owls, arrogant in the temporary absence of crows, hunted in daylight. The rabbits were hidden and the foxes were visible, the chickadees here, the kingfishers gone. The ducks must be gone or dead, but two coots defied reason and clumsy-footed across a blue arena in the dead cattail crowd. Newts, sluggish among under-ice debris, ate comatose insects and kept growing. On the coldest day of the year, they shed their skins as though mid-summer reigned.

Snow became the great democratic leveler, not only in its decorative jousts with the wind, but in its smothering of the grasses, its clothing of the marsh in wool. It fell against the sun which glittered among its crystals and petrified its purpose,

An American coot finds slippery footing on marsh ice, by Robert P. Carr.

Ice-encrusted cattails rise from a frozen marsh (left), by Frank Oberle. A black-capped chickadee (above) perches on a cattail head, by Larry West.

revealed sexagonal bodies, and countless different flake forms radiating from heartlike cores.

The crystals settled and trapped the warmth of both atmosphere and earth. The snow might thaw, then freeze into a crust, but the warm air remained well trapped. Inside the snow, it was possible to laugh at the winter.

—Franklin Russell, 1969

MARSHLAND ELEGY

Our ability to perceive quality in nature begins, as in art, with the pretty. It expands through successive stages of the beautiful to values as yet uncaptured by language. The quality of cranes lies, I think, in this higher gamut, as yet beyond the reach of words.

This much, though, can be said: our appreciation of the crane grows with the slow unraveling of earthly history. His tribe, we now know, stems out of the remote Eocene. The other members of the fauna in which he originated are long since entombed within the hills. When we hear his call we hear no mere bird. We hear the trumpet in the orchestra of evolution. He is the symbol of our untamable past, of that incredible sweep of millennia which underlies and conditions the daily affairs of birds and men.

And so they live and have their being—these cranes—not in the constricted present, but in the wider reaches of evolutionary time. Their annual return is the ticking of the geologic clock. Upon the place of their return they confer a peculiar distinction. Amid the endless mediocrity of the commonplace, a crane marsh holds a paleontological patent of nobility, won in the march of aeons, . . .

—Aldo Leopold, 1949

A muskrat lodge noses above a winter marsh (left), by Lynn M. Stone; a short-tailed weasel returns after a successful hunt (above), by Phil Dotson. A New Mexico marsh (overleaf) welcomes sandhill cranes for the winter, by Robert P. Carr.

DECEMBER 15

WINTER ANIMALS

In the course of the winter I threw out half a bushel of ears of sweet-corn, which had not got ripe, on to the snow crust by my door, and was amused by watching the motions of the various animals which were baited by it. In the twilight and the night the rabbits came regularly and made a hearty meal. All day long the red squirrels came and went, and afforded me much entertainment by their manœuvres. One would approach at first warily through the shrub-oaks, running over the snow crust by fits and starts like a leaf blown by the wind, now a few paces this way, with wonderful speed and waste of energy, making inconceivable haste with his "trotters," as if it were for a wager, and now as many paces that way, but never getting on more than half a rod at a time; and then suddenly pausing with a ludicrous expression and a gratuitous somerset, as if all the eyes in the universe were fixed on him,—for all the motions of a squirrel, even in the most solitary recesses of the forest, imply spectators as much as those of a dancing girl,—wasting more time in delay and circumspection than would have sufficed to walk the whole distance,—I never saw one walk,—and then suddenly, before you could say Jack Robinson, he would be in the top of a young pitch-pine, winding up his clock and chiding all imaginary spectators, soliloquizing and talking to all the universe at the same time,—for no reason that I could ever detect, or he himself was aware of, I suspect. At length he would reach the corn, and selecting a suitable ear, frisk about in the same uncertain trigonometrical way to the top-most stick of my wood-pile, before my window, where he looked me in the face, and there sit for hours, supplying himself with a new ear from time to time, nibbling at first voraciously and throwing the half-naked cobs about; till at length he grew more dainty still and played with his food, tasting only the inside of the kernel, and the ear, which was held balanced over the stick by one paw, slipped from his careless grasp and fell to the ground, when he would look over at it with a ludicrous expression of uncertainty, as if suspecting that it had life, with a mind not made up whether to get it again, or a new one, or be off; now thinking of corn, then listening to hear what was in the wind. So the little impudent fellow would waste many an ear in a forenoon; till at last, seizing some longer and plumper one, considerably bigger than himself, and skilfully balancing it, he would set out with it to the woods, like a tiger with a buffalo, by the same zig-zag course and frequent pauses, scratching along with it as if it were too heavy for him and falling all the while, making its fall a diagonal between a perpendicular and horizontal, being determined to put it through at any rate;—a singularly frivolous and whimsical fellow;—and so he would get off with it to where he lived, perhaps carry it to the top of a pine tree forty or fifty rods distant, and I would afterwards find the cobs strewn about the woods in various directions.

At length the jays arrive, whose discordant screams were heard long before, as they were warily making their approach an eighth of a mile off, and in a stealthy and sneaking manner they flit from tree to tree, nearer and nearer, and pick up the kernels which the squirrels have dropped. Then, sitting on a pitch-pine bough, they attempt to swallow in their haste a kernel which is too big for their throats and chokes them; and after great labor they disgorge it, and spend an hour in the endeavor to crack it by repeated blows with their bills. They were manifestly thieves, and I had not much respect for them; but the squirrels, though at first shy, went to work as if they were taking what was their own.

"Snow Bunny—Cottontail Rabbit," acrylic painting by Nicholas Wilson, 1981.

At feeder distance men and birds have a healthy way of getting along together without ever touching....

— ❋ —

Meanwhile also came the chicadees in flocks, which picking up the crumbs the squirrels had dropped, flew to the nearest twig, and placing them under their claws, hammered away at them with their little bills, as if it were an insect in the bark, till they were sufficiently reduced for their slender throats. A little flock of these tit-mice came daily to pick a dinner out of my wood-pile, or the crumbs at my door, with faint flitting lisping notes, like the tinkling of icicles in the grass, or else with sprightly *day day day,* or more rarely, in spring-like days, a wiry summery *phe-be* from the wood-side. They were so familiar that at length one alighted on an armful of wood which I was carrying in, and pecked at the sticks without fear. I once had a sparrow alight upon my shoulder for a moment while I was hoeing in a village garden, and I felt that I was more distinguished by that circumstance than I should have been by any epaulet I could have worn. The squirrels also grew at last to be quite familiar, and occasionally stepped upon my shoe, when that was the nearest way.

—*Henry David Thoreau, 1854*

FEEDER DIVIDENDS

We feed the birds not so much to save the birds as to bring them closer. That is the whole proposition: the bird must come to *our* table placed where *we* decree if it wants to be saved from cruel winter famine. Conceivably, somewhere, the human being does exist who would be willing to place his or her bird food out in some invisible dispensary, with no guest book, no windows opening upon it, no way to watch arrivals and departures, and no entry at all, for the host, into the endless display of the foibles, virtues, cupidities, affections, graces, and even the occasional nonsense of the guests.

At feeder distance men and birds have a healthy way of getting along together without ever touching—touch, as one thinks of it, is the ultimate token by which we contrive to *own* people and things—that is seldom achieved in relationships with wives, husbands, children, cats, dogs, lovers, or even flowers.

But the ultimate overpowering reason for bribing birds to come closer—the experience that takes the human being back to the feeder again and again as if he or she could never be satiated—is that experience of color that can be provided only by the free and living bird at close range, within ten feet of the natural eye.

A cedar waxwing, gray and indistinguishable in the distance except for its crest, and often, in the reference book, unnaturally garish like color television, becomes an exotic jewel of tints never otherwise manufactured when he lights on a feeder just outside the watcher's window. Many of the colors that reveal themselves when birds can be brought that close are beyond our charts, our pigments, our words, and our senses.

The richest returns often come from species least likely, seen from a distance or from the plates in a book, to be considered especially worthy of invitation. A drab mockingbird, noticed at first only because it has shifted its territory north in recent years, didn't establish a real welcome for itself until, at the feeder the other day, it turned its back, always gray in book or on garden post, and disclosed its real color. It was still gray, no doubt, but with a luminous filtering of brown, a blush of chlorophyll, and a suggestion of low-toned iridescents in a combination—once again words cannot report what the eye thinks it can see.

The most overwhelming sight that could ever come to a feeding station would be the female tanager, which Peterson describes as "dull green above and yellowish below, with brownish or blackish wings." Some of us have been close enough to the female tanager in the fields, on days when her husband was not commanding all our attention, to know that is woeful understatement.

—*Alan Olmstead, 1977*

Songbirds heed the dinner bell at a winter feeding station, by Jim Schmidt.

Children refill a tube feeder,
by R. Y. Kaufman

❋ John James Audubon did it; John Burroughs did it; Henry David Thoreau certainly did it. In the 19th century, luminaries were feeding the birds and writing about it.

There are no known records of America's early settlers feeding birds in their backyards. But since the practice was common in Europe, it is likely that the new Americans kept up the tradition.

The first person credited with starting a planned bird-feeding program was Mrs. E. B. Davenport of Brattleboro, Vermont. In 1896, the enterprising lady set out a variety of feeders and food in her yard.

"I began this work from love of, and companionship of, these feathered friends.... I know of no other pursuit that brings richer rewards," she exclaimed.

Since then, bird feeding in America has become one of America's favorite pastimes, with 60 million folks feeding birds each year.

❋ *Jule Neg:* In Scandinavia, there is an old tradition observed by many farmers: Each year the last sheaf of wheat harvested is bundled up and set aside in the barn. On Christmas Eve, the special *Jule Neg*—Christmas Bundles—are securely attached to a pole out of doors as a treat for birds and other wildlife. Sharing his grain with the animals symbolizes the farmer's hopes for a good

harvest the following year.

The tradition was brought to America, but survived chiefly as a folk story told to children of Scandinavian families.

In 1975 Kurt Krantz, owner of Still Meadow Farms in Minnesota, wanted to encourage the revival of *Jule Neg,* but found it impossible to find the right sort of wheat to make these bundles. Old strains had handsome, long, sturdy stalks. Today, wheat is grown short and with loose tops to accommodate modern farm machinery.

So he asked the University of Minnesota's Agricultural Department for help—together they researched and began to grow an old style of wheat that had not been available since 1930! The next step was to locate old machinery that could harvest his crop. Fortunately, he was able to find three old McCormick reapers—and was in business.

Now, a number of Midwesterners of Swedish descent are keeping the custom of *Jule Neg* alive—enough of them, in fact, to support an entire farm devoted to growing and bundling these special wheat sheaves.

Adapted from *Engwall's Journal,* Fall/Winter 1984

❋ Tips for getting started:

When to feed. If you decide to feed birds in winter, you should stock your feeder before the first cold snap of fall in order to attract customers, and continue well into spring when natural food is again available. Most importantly, if you start, make sure you provide a steady food source, because the birds will come to depend on it.

Where to place feeders. Place feeders on the south side of your house where the birds will be most protected from the wind. If you can, it is also a good idea to set feeders near bushes or trees—the birds can roost in the vegetation and, more importantly, can hide or escape from predators there. Obviously, you will want to place your feeders where you can easily see them. Feeders outside kitchen, living room, or bedroom windows will give you a wonderful show.

What to feed. One of the best ways to lure birds to a new feeder is to scatter broken up white bread. Apparently, birds are drawn to the eye-catching white morsels. Later, switch to other foods. Sunflower seed (oil, black-striped, or hulled) is the most popular with many birds. Other popular foods include: seed mixtures containing millet, canary seed, rape and flax; suet and suet mixtures; thistle seeds for finches and sparrows; and chopped peanuts and other nutmeats. Peanut butter is also a nutritious food, but it should be mixed with suet or cornmeal because it may be difficult for birds to swallow if unmixed.

DECEMBER 16

EL GORDO

During the three years we spent in the Swan Mountains of northwestern Montana, my wife, Beth Ferris, and I stayed with the mountain goats through one complete mountain winter and portions of others. No one else had tried to keep tightly focused on individual mountain goats and their activities from the beginning of this most crucial of seasons to the end. Our efforts at minute-by-minute observation blew away in blizzards, and we were sometimes too busy trying to keep from freezing or getting caught out in avalanche conditions to give any thought at all to what our white neighbors were doing.

Beth and I were carrying a load of gear the final miles uphill toward our Little Creek outpost in the Swans. We had been gone from this camp nearly three weeks and were anxious to catch up with the lives of the members of the goat herd wintering across the valley.

Having chosen to specialize in goatwatching, Beth and I were equally hemmed in by winter. It snowed practically every day at the elevation of our Little Creek camp, sometimes condensing out of a clear sky. Between blizzards, foggy drizzle, and short days, we considered each hour of midwinter data we could collect worth a dozen summer hours and were reluctant to leave our outpost.

So we sat by the telescope in great globs of clothing or reworked data in the tent. I finally got Tolstoy's 800-page *War and Peace* read and enjoyed it both times. The newspapers we packed in to start fires proved almost too valuable as extra reading material to burn. And there is far more to be learned from the labels of soup cans and noodle cartons than most people appreciate.

Well protected against the cold, a mountain goat takes in the sun on a high mountain slope, by Keith Gunnar.

If we looked nearly as wide as we were tall in our layers of wool and down, we were nothing compared to El Gordo, the Completely Symmetrical Shrew. He, or she, started out like any other shrew: trim, hyperactive, following a long mobile snout toward its next meal. As it happened, El Gordo's snout led it through the tent one day and over to the food dish of Kobuk, the Finicky Malemute, our semi-loyal dog. Nirvana! Whether Kobuk had lain and watched snowflakes all day or mushed ten miles behind us carrying his dogpack, he never once finished what was put in his bowl.

For weeks the Return of El Gordo to the trough was prime-time entertainment in the goat camp. Shrews have a metabolism like a miniature nuclear meltdown and need to eat their weight in one thing or another so often they would starve to death if they stopped to catch a few solid hours of sleep. The number of overweight shrews in the world is therefore limited, which tells you something of the devoted effort required on El Gordo's part to inflate to squash ball proportions before abruptly disappearing, never to return.

—Douglas H. Chadwick, 1983

A shrew pokes out of its hollow-log home to search for food, by A. Blank.

THE EVER HUNGRY JAY

In the winter we who live in the country owe a great debt to the birds that consent to come to our bird feeders. Everyone I know has a bird feeder and the action at the feeder is a major source of interest and conversation. Bird-feeding people employ various methods and devices. They have favorite birds and less favorite birds. The differing devices are feeders cleverly designed to let some birds get at the seed and exclude others. The bird most people want to exclude is the blue jay. A blue jay will sit in a bird feeder and swallow one sunflower seed after another as though his stomach were a bottomless pit. He swallows conspicuously. You can see the seed go down and hit bottom—thunk!—and then he gobbles another. While eating he looks rude and complacent—elbows on the table, no suggestion of gratitude. Sunflower seed is the blue jay's special delight—as it is for almost all birds—and it is the most expensive seed commonly fed to birds. I've heard people say they simply couldn't afford to be ripped off by blue jays and so they have bought elaborate contraptions to thwart them. Snowbound and watching birds wistfully, wishing I could sail over the white meadows instead of floundering, I began to think about the economics of bird feeding. I decided to do a little local research with a view to answering such questions as these: Is the blue jay needy or greedy? Is it possible to fill up a blue jay? Do they have other resources, as some of my friends suspect, and simply prefer handouts? What is the cost

A blue jay adds color to a winter day, by Gary Meszaros.

While cracking a sunflower seed, a self-assured blue jay peers from within a feeder, by Harry Hartman.

As I sit here by my window, . . . it is a great vicarious pleasure
to watch a jay drift . . . to my offering of sunflower seeds . . . .

— ❋ —

of sunflower seed and how does this cost relate to the cost of a blue-jay-excluding device?

At the time of my investigation Damon's Hardware in Wakefield, Rhode Island, was selling twelve and a half pounds of sunflower seed for $4.50 and fifty pounds for $14.95. I took ten seeds to the drugstore and had them weighed on an apothecary's scale. With the help of my husband I computed that ten seeds weighing .92 grams equal 3/100 of an ounce. At this rate there are 4,969 seeds to the pound. At $14.95 for fifty pounds, a pound costs about thirty cents. Therefore each seed costs 6/1000 of a cent. In other words, I was able to buy 166 sunflower seeds for a penny.

At home I telephoned a few friends for their views on bird feeding. I am happy to report that everyone took a generous and liberal view of jays.

I also telephoned Lee Gardner, the resident biologist at the Norman Bird Sanctuary in Middletown, Rhode Island, an expert witness on the blue jay. Members of the family Corvidae, jays are related to crows and are indeed smart and aggressive. They will even attack a person in defense of their young. "I've had a jay swoop and rake my head with its claws when I picked a baby up off the ground. They can lick almost any other bird except a mockingbird, which is even tougher. They live just about everywhere east of the Mississippi. It is hard to count them in a locality. They are casually migratory and move here and there with wind and weather. Their flocks are not due to comradeship but because when one jay finds food others follow, so a group will descend first on one bird feeder and then on another."

Gardner confirmed the suspicion that blue jays are among the least needy of all the species in the bird breadline. "They are omnivorous and if seeds fail they can go to the beach and eat a clam or to the dump and eat a dead rat," Gardner said. I asked about their conspicuous gobbling, and he

explained that, like crows, jays are hiders. They fill their crop with seeds, carry them away, and then cough them up. They husk and eat what they want and hide the rest under leaves or in nooks and crannies. Ecologically it is a valuable trait since jays plant seeds that they forget to dig up and thus help to start new growth, but the habit is indeed quite depleting to the sunflower seed supply at bird feeders. Gardner dismissed as unimportant the competition between jays and smaller birds at feeders, provided the seed supply is ample. If there is enough to go around, the small birds simply sit and wait their turn. Thus an alternative to the blue jay baffler is a sufficient supply of seed.

Gardner's information led me back to my financial calculations. After a half hour of watching jays swallow sunflower seeds, I arrived at a maximum of twenty-five seeds in one sitting. A jay flying away with twenty-five seeds is carrying off 15/100 of a penny's worth. A flock of ten jays is making off with one and a half cents' worth. If they do this three times a day, the cost is four and a half cents. Let's be generous and give them a nickel a day. I am happy that I have come upon this information. As I sit here by my window, aware that if I go out in the tempting, treacherous snow my feet will feel heavy and cold in no time, it is a great vicarious pleasure to watch a jay drift effortlessly from branch to branch—and thence to my offering of sunflower seeds, spread out on an open feeder available to all. I can watch him gobble his twenty-five-seed capacity with an easy mind. At 15/100 of a penny the sight is a real bargain. It gives me a feeling that is rare these days. It makes me feel terribly rich.

—Faith McNulty, 1980

DECEMBER 17

CHRISTMAS SPRUCE

Armed with saw and hatchet, we venture to mingle with the crowd of spruce on the terrace. The blue-green ranks are thick on the slope, the million bristly fingers of their branches interlocked in a dense barrier against blundering invasion. And invasion, let it be known, is why we came; to claim payment for the rental of this slope by a generation of trees and those that dwell within the thicket. It is a large community—mouse and rabbit, chickadee and nuthatch and junco, a hundred kinds of bug and beetle in season—for owl and crow cannot penetrate the formation. Even pussycats must slither along the ground and then be caught and caught again by the brittle triggers of the dead branches lowest on the trunks.

In summer it is cool and moist beneath this shade. And now at Christmas it is warm—warm, at least, by any ready comparison afield. The wind gushes, snow laden, from the northwest, but the spruce only sigh, the candles of the last year bending. Within the thicket the snow loses its velocity and sifts gently down upon the duff. All this, of course, is among the reasons the spruce grow here. They were planted not so long ago on this barren ground to generate a thriving village. They have done so and have further flourished to the point where they can serve a more selfish purpose for their landlord.

They crowd so thickly upon one another now that it is time for some to go, that the others may grow still larger. This, too, was planned, so the needful thinning should coincide with the yule-tide. Thus the landlord might do as he did when he was young, a hundred years ago, and cut his own Christmas tree again on his own acreage, not only propitiating his ego but causing the shades of the old tree-worshipping ancestors to draw close to the edge of the firelight in the living room and smile. There is time, while growing spruce trees from seedlings to ten feet high, to conjure on such things.

But master plans often go awry for the very reason of their complexity; they take so long to execute. The children battle with me against the closeness of the spruce grove. A tree of suitable height is singled out, sawed, and hauled free from its clutching companions. But once it is free, the triumph dims. The boys look on the prize with dismay. There is a brown platform of dead branches at the bottom, a great vacancy where a strong brother stifled the growth on this side, a crookedness where ice tipped a leader and another took over, a clear gap in the middle testifying to splendid growth in a wet, warm spring.

My sons are the soul of courtesy, under the circumstances, but the message is plain: I have spent fifteen years courting this dismal prize while one infinitely superior can be purchased from the smirking profiteer on the corner for a little cash and no effort at all. So be it. Sometimes defeat comes easy. The young judge with a deadly eye, and tradition is no substitute these days for quality.

—*Dion Henderson, 1979*

"Out for Christmas Trees," oil painting by Grandma Moses, 1946.

A CHRISTMAS MEMORY

Morning. Frozen rime lusters the grass; the sun, round as an orange and orange as hot-weather moons, balances on the horizon, burnishes the silvered winter woods. A wild turkey calls. A renegade hog grunts in the undergrowth. Soon, by the edge of knee-deep, rapid-running water, we have to abandon the buggy. Queenie wades the stream first, paddles across barking complaints at the swiftness of the current, the pneumonia-making coldness of it. We follow, holding our shoes and equipment (a hatchet, a burlap sack) above our heads. A mile more: of chastising thorns, burs and briers that catch at our clothes; of rusty pine needles brilliant with gaudy fungus and molted feathers. Here, there, a flash, a flutter, an ecstasy of shrillings remind us that not all the birds have flown south. Always, the path unwinds through lemony sun pools and pitch-black vine tunnels. Another creek to cross: a disturbed armada of speckled trout froths the water round us, and frogs the size of plates practice belly flops; beaver workmen are building a dam. On the farther shore, Queenie shakes herself and trembles. My friend shivers, too: not with cold but enthusiasm. One of her hat's ragged roses sheds a petal as she lifts her head and inhales the

pine-heavy air. "We're almost there; can you smell it, Buddy?" she says, as though we were approaching an ocean.

And, indeed, it is a kind of ocean. Scented acres of holiday trees, prickly-leafed holly. Red berries shiny as Chinese bells: black crows swoop upon them screaming. Having stuffed our burlap sacks with enough greenery and crimson to garland a dozen windows, we set about choosing a tree. "It should be," muses my friend, "twice as tall as a boy. So a boy can't steal the star." The one we pick is twice as tall as me. A brave handsome brute that survives thirty hatchet strokes before it keels with a creaking rending cry. Lugging it like a kill, we commence the long trek out. Every few yards we abandon the struggle, sit down and pant. But we have the strength of triumphant huntsmen; that and the tree's virile, icy perfume revive us, goad us on. Many compliments accompany our sunset return along the red clay road to town; but my friend is sly and noncommittal when passers-by praise the treasure perched in our buggy: what a fine tree and where did it come from? "Yonderways," she murmurs vaguely. Once a car stops and the rich mill owner's lazy wife leans out and whines: "Giveya two-bits cash for that ol tree." Ordinarily my friend is afraid of saying no; but on this occasion she promptly shakes her head: "We wouldn't take a dollar." The mill owner's wife persists. "A dollar, my foot! Fifty cents. That's my last offer. Goodness, woman, you can get another one." In answer, my friend gently reflects: "I doubt it. There's never two of anything."

—*Truman Capote, 1956*

Hauling the Christmas tree from the woods, by Kent and Donna Dannen.

"Gathering Christmas Greens,"
engraving c. 1876

❄ If you want to cut your own tree from a National Forest, call your local National Forest office before you set out. Most National Forests prohibit Christmas-tree cutting, although some in every region of the country do allow it. Anyone cutting a tree from these forests must acquire a permit from the Forest Service.

❄ Whether you opt for the pleasure of cutting your own tree or the convenience of buying a ready-cut one, your choice will be easier if you know something about evergreens. Pines and firs, for example, retain their needles longest; with care, spruces will keep their needles for about ten to twelve days.

Douglas Fir

A native of the West Coast, this evergreen has short, soft needles that won't prick your hands as you decorate the branches. This makes it a particularly good tree in households with children. However, this tree's limber branches may sag with too many or too heavy decorations.

Balsam Fir

Common throughout the East, this tree also has soft, rounded needles; the Balsam Fir's branches will also hold many ornaments without sagging. An added benefit: This evergreen has a delightful aroma.

Scotch Pine

Originally brought from Europe, this tree is now widely planted in North America. Proper trimming and pruning give it a bushy, perfect Christmas-tree shape. The blue green Scotch Pine has excellent needle retention.

Eastern Red Cedar

Found throughout the eastern half of the country, this tree grows best in limestone regions. It has a dense pyramidal crown.

White Pine

This is the largest conifer of the Northeast, growing 75 to 100 feet tall and 2 to 4 feet in diameter. The tree is topped by a pyramidal crown of whorled horizontal branches and has good needle retention.

Norway Spruce

Originally an imported tree from Europe, the Norway Spruce is now widely planted in the U.S. and Canada. It can grow to a height of 125 feet. Its needles are dark green, flattened to triangular.

Douglas Fir

Balsam Fir

Scotch Pine

Eastern Red Cedar

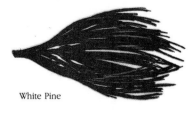

White Pine

Norway Spruce

DECEMBER 18

LAND OF DECEMBER

In our part of the world, December is the time when winter gets down to business. For a month or more, there have been ambiguous hints and harbingers. Plunging nocturnal temperatures are followed by Indian summer days in late October. Hard frosts wither the last of the squash vines in the November garden, but along dirt roads already solid as iron and cold as death, the autumn color still flares tantalizingly here and there. Then December puts a stop to all of this, muffling the earth under a deep and unequivocal snowfall.

Winter is a *serious* business up here in northern Vermont. It forces all of us to change our habits. For the human population, at least that part of it represented by our small family, the process is fairly simple. We get up earlier, dress ourselves and our children more warmly, carry blankets, snow shovels, buckets of sand and booster cables in the back of the car, drink hot soup at lunch time and go about our business.

For the animals in our environment, it is more complicated. The deer who wandered freely through our pastures and the old orchard in early November, sampling frostbitten alfalfa shoots and a final scattering of apples shaken to the ground by autumn winds, are no longer to be seen. This first storm has confined them to their wintering "yards" in swamp or forest, and their survival from now on will hinge largely upon the weather. Will they be able to travel freely enough to find food for all, or will they be limited to one browsing area, a fate which assures the starvation of many? Will the snow be deep enough, on the other hand, to discourage marauding dogs from entering their feeding grounds and killing off the weaker animals?

Others, lucky or not according to your perspective, are fed by us. Flocks of sparrows, chickadees, nuthatches, woodpeckers and grosbeaks who abandoned us for the summer now congregate at the feeders, hoping we will not forget them. In the

In winter, Stowe, Vermont, takes on a Christmas-card look, by Clyde H. Smith.

barn, the cows and sheep, the goats and ducks, the geese and chickens all make anxious bids for our attention, each in its own manner.

Feeding a dozen barnyard animals is one gift-giving activity to which there are absolutely no strings attached, except for the baling twine. I count that a blessing.

There are still other, unexpected blessings to be had at this time of year. We come upon them with surprised appreciation as our own perspective changes, now that the season has truly enveloped us. The snow itself, which loomed as a threat for so long before it actually made its appearance, now reveals itself in the character of a gift.

The children are the first to recognize this and to delight in it. They plunge into the new element as if it were a summer ocean, with happy abandon. They make snow forts, snow angels, snowmen and snowwomen of every imaginable size and variety. We ourselves take a little longer to adjust. We wait for a clear day, strap on snowshoes or skis, and find that parts of the landscape which were all but forbidden to us during hunting season and unpleasant to wade through during the rains of late fall are newly accessible.

As in a dream, we pass unaccompanied through pastures alive with curious Holsteins in the summer, glide unseen across our neighbor's empty

Often there is a thaw around Christmastime,
and the brook runs freely for a while.

hayfields and the sugar woods where we will be tapping trees in March, move unimpeded, thanks to the smooth snow now covering it, over an unused field grown so thick with ground hemlock that you could not negotiate it comfortably at any other time of year. The land is ours again.

Indoors, we discover the gift of centering, of drawing into our own family core. The snowdrifts close in around us, night falls earlier, and the family necessarily spends more time together—usually in the kitchen, the coziest room in the house. We read more stories aloud, play more games, become involved in baking Christmas cookies, making popcorn and other holiday projects. By the end of February, we may be at each other's throats in a frenzy of cabin fever, but now we are content to be caught up in the festivity of togetherness, at this most festive season.

In our town, we have caroling on Christmas Eve. A candlelight service is held in the Congregational Church, as it is in other churches throughout the country and the world on the same night. Not many churches were built in as poignantly picturesque a Christmas setting as ours, I suspect, and not many towns have the Christmas-card look of the northern New England hill towns of our area in December, with their white clapboard houses and white church spires. You may even see a woodsman with a horse and heavy sled, pulling logs out of the woods at the outskirts of town, giving the whole scene the look of a Currier and Ives print.

When I travel the old logging roads on my skis, I like to see who has been here before me: two fat-pawed back footprints of a snowshoe hare overtake the delicate smaller prints of the front feet in a repetitive pattern across my trail, while the long, light line of doglike paw marks left by a red fox traverses our meadow, and I can see the tiny traces of a mouse's feet and tail, exploring the roots of a large tamarack as I turn the corner of the trail that leads to the brook.

Often there is a thaw around Christmastime, and the brook runs freely for a while. Then I will see many more tracks: deep marks of deer; light prints that might belong to a fisher our dog treed in this area earlier in the fall; and once a puzzling troughlike trail lined with small prints close together, which our woods-wise neighbor identified as the low-bodied porcupine's characteristic winter track. But even if there is no thaw, the few animal tracks that are visible will all lead to one small hole where the brook runs fastest and deepest, a place where the ice has a hard time covering up.

At this very spot, I lost a tin cup to a Christmas impulse. I used to carry the cup when I went cross-country skiing in order to refresh myself at the brook. One holiday afternoon, I hung it on a broken spruce branch that protrudes above the brook, just in case anyone else should need it. Probably it was a futile gesture. But I figured that you never can tell who might be passing through this part of the world in December, thirsty enough to appreciate a cup full of water and good will.

—*Reeve L. Brown, 1979*

A skier ponders a creek
crossing, by Frank S. Balthis.

DECEMBER 19

A HILLSIDE THAW

To think to know the country and not know
The hillside on the day the sun lets go
Ten million silver lizards out of snow!
As often as I've seen it done before
I can't pretend to tell the way it's done.
It looks as if some magic of the sun
Lifted the rug that bred them on the floor
And the light breaking on them made them run.
But if I thought to stop the wet stampede,
And caught one silver lizard by the tail,
And put my foot on one without avail,
And threw myself wet-elbowed and wet-kneed
In front of twenty others' wriggling speed,—
In the confusion of them all aglitter,
And birds that joined in the excited fun
By doubling and redoubling song and twitter,
I have no doubt I'd end by holding none.

It takes the moon for this. The sun's a wizard
By all I tell; but so's the moon a witch.
From the high west she makes a gentle cast
And suddenly, without a jerk or twitch,
She has her spell on every single lizard.
I fancied when I looked at six o'clock
The swarm still ran and scuttled just as fast.
The moon was waiting for her chill effect.
I looked at nine: the swarm was turned to rock
In every lifelike posture of the swarm,
Transfixed on mountain slopes almost erect.
Across each other and side by side they lay.
The spell that so could hold them as they were
Was wrought through trees without a breath of storm
To make a leaf, if there had been one, stir.
It was the moon's: she held them until day,
One lizard at the end of every ray.
The thought of my attempting such a stay!

—Robert Frost, 1923

Birch trees reflected on an ice
floe, by R. Hamilton Smith.

114

A striped skunk (above) makes a winter foray, by Don and Pat Valenti. A meadow vole (opposite) peers from its winter runway, by John Shaw.

WARMTH IN MIDWINTER

Each year, after the midwinter blizzards, there comes a night of thaw when the tinkle of dripping water is heard in the land. It brings strange stirrings, not only to creatures abed for the night, but to some who have been asleep for the winter. The hibernating skunk, curled up in his deep den, uncurls himself and ventures forth to prowl the wet world, dragging his belly in the snow. His track marks one of the earliest datable events in that cycle of beginnings and ceasings which we call a year.

The track is likely to display an indifference to mundane affairs uncommon at other seasons; it leads straight across-country, as if its maker had hitched his wagon to a star and dropped the reins.

Each year, ... there comes a night of thaw
when the tinkle of dripping water is heard in the land.

— ❄ —

I follow, curious to deduce his state of mind and appetite, and destination if any . . . .

A meadow mouse, startled by my approach, darts damply across the skunk track. Why is he abroad in daylight? Probably because he feels grieved about the thaw. Today his maze of secret tunnels, laboriously chewed through the matted grass under the snow, are tunnels no more, but only paths exposed to public view and ridicule. Indeed the thawing sun has mocked the basic premises of the microtine economic system!

The mouse is a sober citizen who knows that grass grows in order that mice may store it as underground haystacks, and that snow falls in order that mice may build subways from stack to stack: supply, demand, and transport all neatly organized. To the mouse, snow means freedom from want and fear.

A rough-legged hawk comes sailing over the meadow ahead. Now he stops, hovers like a king-fisher, and then drops like a feathered bomb into the marsh. He does not rise again, so I am sure he has caught, and is now eating, some worried mouse-engineer who could not wait until night to inspect the damage to his well-ordered world.

The rough-leg has no opinion why grass grows, but he is well aware that snow melts in order that hawks may again catch mice. He came down out of the Arctic in the hope of thaws, for to him a thaw means freedom from want and fear. . . .

The skunk track leads on, showing no interest in possible food, and no concern over the rompings or retributions of his neighbors. I wonder what he has on his mind; what got him out of bed? Can one impute romantic motives to this corpulent fellow, dragging his ample beltline through the slush? Finally the track enters a pile of driftwood, and does not emerge. I hear the tinkle of dripping water among the logs, and I fancy the skunk hears it too. I turn homeward, still wondering.

—Aldo Leopold, 1949

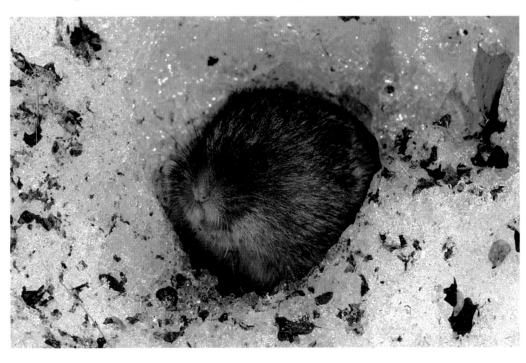

WHEN CLOCKS GO WRONG

It is true that December is, most often, a winter month of cold and darkness and storm, when hibernating wildlings sleep the deep sleep of winter torpor, and non-hibernating creatures move warily, hampered by the weather, amid their hungry predators.

But sometimes a wintry December brings, also, a day or even a week of surprising gentleness, of sunshine and blue skies, of temperatures that rise above fifty degrees Fahrenheit—especially on dark tree trunks and in sheltered places that face the southward sun. And because of that magical measure of heat some biological clocks go off too soon; some little creatures are triggered into activity when they should be lying low, and lives are lost as nature weeds out another lot of living things with poor survival habits.

For some animals the warmth is merely a welcome reprieve from the winter's cold and they hunt or flee in greater comfort, but they break no laws. Their clocks have not gone wrong.

On warm and gentle December days chipmunks come up from their dark bedrooms and race about in the dry leaves on the woods floor, and gray squirrels dash playfully along lofty highways. Cottontails and white-tailed deer skitter and prance on their own hidden pathways in the hours of dawn and of twilight; and opossums, raccoons, foxes and skunks prowl comfortably through the night.

There are others, though, enjoying the warmth and freedom, whose stories end quite differently.

Today, . . . I saw a blue-edged mourning cloak butterfly
drifting down a sunlit corridor as though spring were here.

— ❄ —

For three days now the red line on the thermometer outside my window has touched the bar marked fifty, and has sometimes pushed several degrees beyond that mark before the close of day.

Today, as I walked through the woods, I saw a blue-edged mourning cloak butterfly drifting down a sunlit corridor as though spring were here. It is using energy, consuming its little store of fuel, and there is not a sap-bleeding tree in all this December woods, not a drop of food to re-fill that dark butterfly body.

Out on the hilltop, beyond the woods, a bright yellow common sulphur butterfly danced across the old hayfield looking as cheerfully at home as though the sun-sparkled brown world were filled with clover blossoms. Common sulphurs usually hibernate as pupae, protected from winter weather by the hard shell of the chrysalis; and only sometimes, and only perhaps, hibernate successfully as adults. This one, with a biological clock so faulty that it split its shell and emerged from its chrysalis in December, is obviously going to have to hibernate as an adult or, most likely, to die in the attempt. There is no food, now, for a little body that feeds upon the nectars of the clover family.

Over-wintering female wasps, and houseflies, and ladybugs come creeping out of the cracks and crannies where they have successfully sheltered thus far, and fly about or sun themselves on the south side of the house; and I will find their frozen bodies lying on the stones in little windrows when the weather changes back to winter.

Lilacs and forsythia often put forth a few blossoms if the weather stays warm enough for long enough. We almost expect it of them. But in the orchard this afternoon I found two pink and white blossoms on the red astrakhan apple tree. They were as fresh and as fragrant as any blooms of May-time, and a honeybee from a nearby hive rolled among their stamens.

The honeybee probably got back to its hive with the pollen it collected, but the apple blossoms are doomed. They can never develop a fruit, never set a seed. Nature has no more use for a Maryland apple orchard that blossoms in December than she has for a hornet that attempts a paper cone out of season.

—Mary Leister, 1976

On a day of thaw, a white-tailed deer (opposite) laps melted snow, by Olive Glasgow; a mourning cloak butterfly (above) basks in the sun, by Susan and John Shaw.

DECEMBER 20

BARRED OWL

In the deepest snows, the path which I used from the highway to my house, about half a mile long, might have been represented by a meandering dotted line, with wide intervals between the dots. For a week of even weather I took exactly the same number of steps, and of the same length, coming and going, stepping deliberately and with the precision of a pair of dividers in my own deep tracks,—to such routine the winter reduces us,—yet often they were filled with heaven's own blue. But no weather interfered fatally with my walks, or rather my going abroad, for I frequently tramped eight or ten miles through the deepest snow to keep an appointment with a beech-tree, or a yellow-birch, or an old acquaintance among the pines; when the ice and snow causing their limbs to droop, and so sharpening their tops, had changed the pines into fir-trees; wading to the tops of the highest hills when the snow was nearly two feet deep on a level, and shaking down another snowstorm on my head at every step; or sometimes creeping and floundering thither on my hands and knees, when the hunters had gone into winter quarters. One afternoon I amused myself by watching a barred owl (*Strix nebulosa*) sitting on one of the lower dead limbs of a white-pine, close to the trunk, in broad daylight, I standing within a rod of him. He could hear me when I moved and cronched the snow with my feet, but could not plainly see me. When I made most noise he would stretch out his neck, and erect his neck feathers, and open his eyes wide; but their lids soon fell again, and he began to nod. I too felt a slumberous influence after watching him half an hour, as he sat thus with his eyes half open, like a cat, winged brother of the cat. There was only a narrow slit left between their lids, by which he preserved a peninsular relation to me; thus, with half-shut eyes, looking out from the land of dreams, and endeavoring to realize me, vague object or mote that interrupted his visions. At length, on some louder noise or my nearer approach, he would grow uneasy and sluggishly turn about on his perch, as if impatient at having his dreams disturbed; and when he launched himself off and flapped through the pines, spreading his wings to unexpected breadth, I could not hear the slightest sound from them. Thus, guided amid the pine boughs rather by a delicate sense of their neighborhood than by sight, feeling his twilight way as it were with his sensitive pinions, he found a new perch, where he might in peace await the dawning of his day.

—*Henry David Thoreau, 1854*

Holding its dinner, a barred owl peers from its evergreen perch, by Gary Meszaros.

AN ARCTIC VISITOR

In one or two winters of every decade, the mice in the meadow meet a new predator. From the arctic tundras, a great many snowy owls move south. Perhaps the supply of lemmings in the Far North is unseasonably small. In the Oyster River valley of southeastern New Hampshire the stately white owls take up solitary stations on the snow for daytime hunting. They appear to squint, by raising the feathers around their eyes until only a slanting slit remains to see through. Toward dusk, each owl relaxes again. Its feathers settle back, exposing the whole circles of its big golden eyes.

For the arctic owl, the snow provides a natural background, one against which the bird disappears at any time of day. Often, however, an owl settles in the top of an apple tree overlooking the meadow, and peers from this vantage point over the substitute tundra. Any other owl perched so conspicuously would soon attract a mob of crows. But not the snowy! Any crow that pauses for a close look beats a hasty retreat as soon as the owl spreads its great white wings—as much as sixty-six inches from tip to tip—and lunges at its black tormentor. Smart crows escape. Small birds seldom come close, and the snowy owl seems unaware of them. Domestic pigeons too appear to mean nothing to this regal visitor from the Far North. But any herring gull that settles on the meadow near a mousing owl seldom gets away. Perhaps this is because gulls in the Arctic menace the eggs and nestlings of owls breeding there, as they do also those of many waterfowl.

—Lorus and Margery Milne, 1963

Once the goshawk streaked down, making a pass at a gray squirrel leaping among the upper limbs.

— ❋ —

LORD OF THE YARD

For three years in succession, we were visited in the heart of winter by what was probably the same beautiful blue-gray hawk. Larger than a crow, the largest of the accipiters, it was a goshawk coming down from the northern woods. Each time it remained about three weeks. Its favorite perch was in the top of the highest hickory across the lane. Birds know their hawks. This was demonstrated dramatically by the reaction of the bluejays. For now there was no bragging, no taunting chorus of screams such as greet smaller and slower hawks. Silently the jays melted away or perched motionless deep among the twisted branches of the apple tree. Once the goshawk streaked down, making a pass at a gray squirrel leaping among the upper limbs. Not a jay flew. But they all, in a wave of movement, shifted their position slightly. So far as we could determine the goshawk caught only one jay. It picked it from the air and returned to its perch in the hickory tree, letting the feathers fall to the ground as it fed. For more than an hour after the hawk had left, the tree swarmed with bluejays, screaming, flying from limb to limb, peering down at the scattered feathers below.

In a few days after the goshawk first appeared, the number of jays at Trail Wood, our farm in Connecticut, dropped by half. And of the more than 160 mourning doves that had been feeding daily in our driveway, only four—probably resident birds that nested here—remained. All the rest came back no more that year. The danger was too great around our ample food.

—*Edwin Way Teale, 1974*

Oil paintings by Charles Fracé: "Snowy Owls," 1978 (opposite); "Northern Goshawk," 1972 (above).

They come to Alaska's Chilkat River by the thousands, some from as far away as Washington State. Every winter the stretch of the waterway known as the "Council Grounds" greets almost as many bald eagles as exist throughout the entire lower 48 states.

They come for the fishing; and the fishing here is very good. The Chilkat River run—the latest salmon run in Alaska—provides badly needed winter food for the eagles.

An Alaskan bald eagle strikes a regal pose (left), by Art Wolfe. Along Alaska's Chilkat River, bald eagles congregate by the thousands (above), by George Herben.

DECEMBER 21

BLIZZARD

All Americans have heard of that simoon of the snow—a northwestern blizzard. But, unless they have travelled in the far Northwest, they can never have experienced one; for a blizzard takes place only in a land of intense cold where there is a level, unforested, unbroken, open waste of snow.

During this, our first winter, my brothers and I were very naturally looking out for the terrors of a blizzard. Time wore on into the Christmas season; the snow lay deep and deeper on the ground, and the thermometer was steadily below zero; but there was no great disturbance to note.

One day, however, it came on to blow hard—as hard as I had ever seen it in Ontario. The wavy expanse of snow was tossed into heaps—each heap like a curled but stable wave—and over the crest, in gusty bursts, the wind sent hissing clouds of snow, which hid from view objects a mile off, and left but smoky outlines of those nearer. It was also very cold; and to the newcomers it seemed a hard day indeed. As we watched the snow-sea being tossed about, one of us asked my oldest brother: "Arthur, is this a *blizzard?*"

A contemptuous "Pah!" was the only reply.

A harder, fiercer storm came on us. The thermometer had fallen thirty degrees below zero. All night the winds worked around the house and over the prairie, trampling and tossing the fine powdery snow in wild sport. Fences were quickly disappearing beneath the fast-accumulating heaps; and yet in places the hard grinding of the storm was laying bare the ground. The air was full of snow for fifty feet up. We could not see a hundred yards with clearness. The cold was driven into our faces, so that an hour or more outside necessitated

A blizzard blurs a Wyoming home, by Jonathan T. Wright.

a return to the house to thaw out a nose or an ear. Travelling was impossible; and, as we looked at the careering clouds of snowdust, one said:

"Arthur, *this* is a blizzard, at any rate."

The answer was a disdainful snorted, "Naw."

One day, dawn showed a cloudy sky; and, though the weather seemed calm, there was at times a gust of wind which raised a cloud of snow for a minute, and then let it settle again.

Toward night the wind came up, blowing from the north, and the thermometer had fallen to forty degrees below zero. Later on the wind increased to a gale, and snow fell steadily. All night we heard the sound of the strong wind and the snow hissing over the roof.

Toward morning it grew worse. When it should have been day, we looked out; but nothing was visible at twenty feet. There was naught but a chaos of whirling powdery snow—a steady blast of howling, stinging snow—snow above, snow around, snow below, snow everywhere—snow driven almost through you, bearing a numbing chill to your very bones. The racing clouds were swept low to earth, and whisked along like ice in a torrent. Around the house the wind fairly screamed; every hair-like crack in roof or wall became a funnel for sifted snow. Twenty feet away from the buildings one seemed to be alone in space; even one's feet were hidden in hissing snow; while the terrific gale, chilled to forty degrees below zero, was grinding up solid drifts and hurling their fragments high into the gloom.

The roar was deafening, like the steady r-r-r-r of a fan-blast. The air was like flame on one's flesh through its very coldness. The universe seemed blotted out. There seemed neither heaven nor earth—nothing but furious winds and driving snow—gloom and terrible frost. The day was darkened and the sun forgotten. The world itself seemed blotted out in the awful tumult....

I can say no more! "Storm" is a weak word to describe it. For two days it lasted, and we lived hidden. The third morning came, with calm; it was over. The face of the plains was changed.

As we dug out the cattle, I said: "Arthur! *That was* a blizzard anyhow."

This time there was no reply!

The icy coating on each window pane grew thicker and denser as winter wore on. Nothing was visible through the glass. Nearly every day and all night the hiss and grinding of the blizzard wind showed us how wise were those birds that southwards fled for winter, and those beasts that retreated far underground and slept away the long hard peril of the cold.

Yet there was one little bird that never once seemed to be afraid—the snowbird, the snow-bunting. All winter he was seen about our barns, roosting in holes, burrowing deep into a snow-bank when the feeble sun went down, and living on the waste of the stable—fed, warm and happy.

—*Ernest Thompson Seton, 1940*

— ❄ —

For most birds, prairie winters are much too harsh to endure. By the time the howling blizzards descend on this land, most birds have migrated to milder, southern climes. Not so the snow bunting.

For this denizen of the arctic, the severe prairie is a comparatively mild wintering ground. Also known as "snowflakes" or "snowbirds," these hardy birds fly around in large flocks in the midst of blizzards. Snow buntings can withstand a chilling temperature of -55°F in the open. When the temperature dips further, the birds burrow in the snow for warmth.

WINTER CURTAIN

The first snows on the tallgrass prairie cover even the muted November afterfreeze colors and wipe the slate clean. They blow down in a fury out of a storm born in Canada, come on down the Dakotas, and hit the Flint Hills near the time of Thanksgiving. During a snowstorm, the horizon, so much a part of the prairie in other seasons, is blotted out, so that earth and sky, instead of constantly sparring with each trying to outdo the other in brilliance and color, become one. Land and sky are indistinguishable until the storm passes, and once again the shining, clear-blue dome reigns now over a crystal, cold-white world.

—*Patricia Duncan, 1978*

DECEMBER 22

ON A WEASEL'S TRAIL

I took the trail to the river because I wanted to see open water again after nothing but solid ice on the lakes, brittle frozen brush, and snow that felt like sand. I wanted to see something moving and alive and listen to the gurgle of water as it rippled its way around the rocks of some open place that had never quite closed.

The snow was unbroken, and the jack pines were so heavily laden that their branches touched the ground. Not a sign of life anywhere until I approached the river and saw the delicate twin tracks of a weasel weaving in and out of the underbrush. The tracks disappeared at the base of a protruding stub—gateway, I knew, to the jungle of grass and duff underneath and the meadow mice that lived there. Then for twenty feet there was no sign until the tracks emerged through a tiny hole in the snow and continued on in a straight line to the open water.

I skied to the very edge of the riffle and stood there, feasting my eyes and ears. Moving water after thirty or forty below when the whole world had seemed a frozen crystal of blue and white was an exciting thing.

It was then I saw the weasel standing on a log just below me. Snake-like in shape, this tiny bit of venom was less than a foot in length. Totally white with a faint tinge of yellow, the only contrast the jet-black tip of its tail and its beady eyes, the little animal watched me intently. Then it ran out to the end of the log extending into the water and stood there with one foot uplifted as though wondering whether to plunge in and make it to the other side or retrace its steps and face me.

I sucked softly on the back of my hand, making a sound like the squeak of a meadow mouse. Instantly it turned and looked at me long and steadily, a picture of perfect control and poise. Again I squeaked. Throwing caution to the winds, the weasel dove for the end of the log and in a moment was circling the place where I stood.

How impossible for any small creature to escape such speed and fluid grace, how hopeless to try and run from those smoothly rippling muscles, those sharp black eyes! Suddenly the weasel popped out within a foot of my skis and gave me a wholly malevolent look as though knowing of my deception; then in a flash it was speeding down a fresh rabbit runway through the alders.

There is poetry in the way a weasel can flow through a maze of branches and grass—the liquid movement, the perfect control that enables it to live off those less agile than itself.

—Sigurd F. Olson, 1957

A short-tailed weasel pops out from its evergreen cover near Thunder Bay, Ontario, by Wayne Lankinen.

Even in deep winter, river otters remain playful and active: Undaunted by floating ice chunks, an otter frolics in a river (above), by Michael S. Quinton; another (left) plies one of Yellowstone's waterways, by C. C. Lockwood.

DISPLAYS OF SKILL: OTTER

The numbing cold, the winter-water, waiting,
And I an otter lost in the brisk soft snow.
I have short legs so cannot speed but slide,
I bounce, bounce, undulating for some miles
Then dash, plunge, give myself into the water.

—Ruth Herschberger, 1969

"EVIL ONE"

The Wolverine is a tremendous character. No one can approach the subject of his life and habits, without feeling the same sort of embarrassment one would feel in writing of Cromwell or Tamerlane. Here, we know, is a personality of unmeasured force, courage, and achievement, but so enveloped in mists of legend, superstition, idolatry, fear, and hatred, that one scarcely knows how to begin or what to accept as fact.

Picture a Weasel—and most of us can do that, for we have met that little demon of destruction, that small atom of insensate courage, that symbol-

*The wolverine is a tremendous character . . . a personality of
unmeasured force, courage, and achievement . . . .*

— ❄ —

This wolverine's benign expression (left) belies the creature's courage and steely determination, by Stephen J. Krasemann. An agile climber, a wolverine scales a tree (right), by Jack Couffer.

of slaughter, sleeplessness, and tireless, incredible activity—picture that scrap of demoniac fury, multiply that mite some fifty times, and you have the likeness of a Wolverine.

He is not an animal—that I was assured in my earliest days of hearing his name. He is the Evil One, the Indian Devil, the lost soul of a great hunter, whose only pleasure now is pursuing other hunters, and plaguing them unto madness, till, in some weird way, they strike a bargain with him, and join his company of the damned.

—Ernest Thompson Seton, 1926

THE WILY WOLVERINE

By a wonderful sagacity, [the wolverine] will ascend a tree, and fling from the boughs a species of moss which Elks and Rein[deer] are very fond of; and when those animals come beneath to feed on it, will fall on them and destroy them: or, like the Lynx, it ascends to the boughs of trees, and falls on the Deer which casually pass beneath it, and adheres till they fall down with fatigue.

—*Thomas Pennant, 1784.*

— ❊ —

Maurice Hornocker, scientific adviser to the National Wildlife Federation's Institute for Wildlife Research and the leader of the first long-term wolverine study, thinks it is highly unlikely that wolverines bait their prey with moss. It would take a "pretty smart wolverine," he says. Besides, Hornocker's research showed the creature to be a fairly inefficient hunter that depends mostly on carrion for food.

But if the "Indian devil" came up short on wiliness in its hunting technique, Hornocker and his team of biologists found it remarkable nonetheless. Wolverines, for one, traveled far more widely in winter than any other animal the biologists had studied. Neither high mountain ranges nor large rivers seemed to confine the species. Some individuals traveled up to forty miles in three days.

Furthermore, the wolverine's fabled strength was also confirmed by the scientists. One wolverine caught in a trap within the study area pulled off the jaws from the trap frame. And on another occasion, two wolverines held in chain-link-wire enclosures managed to tear the metal with their teeth and almost make a getaway.

At the end of his study, Hornocker had only words of praise for the wolverine. "From our study, we gained tremendous respect for the animal's tenacity, determination, strength and endurance. Flying over the highest snow-swept peaks of our study area in midwinter and seeing a set of wolverine tracks going straight up and over, we could only look at each other and marvel. No other animal I know of is capable of that. It's small wonder the Eskimos and Indians regarded it as supernatural."

"Window Into Ontario,"
acrylic painting by Robert
Bateman, 1977.

THE JAUNTY BLUE JAY

On the sunny side of a ridge I stopped to rest, for the snow was deep and not well packed. There I discovered that I was not alone. A blue jay flew across an opening before me, a streak of blue flame against the glistening white. He perched in an aspen nearby, where I could admire his black highwayman's mask, his black and white wing bars, his vivid, icy blue. He gave a hard, brazen call, more of a challenge than a song, a challenge to the storm and cold. There was jauntiness and fortitude, announcing to me and to the whole frozen world that where there is wine and sparkle in the air, it is joy to be alive. I liked that jay and what he stood for. No softness there, pure hardiness and disregard of the elements.

The blue jay called again and I caught one brilliant glimpse as he flashed beneath the trees. Gay and cocksure as ever, he had no cares or worries as to his place in the wilderness. For him there was no calm resignation or concern with peace. Whether or not he survived today, this moment he would tell the world what he thought and challenge all comers, including the snow and cold.

—Sigurd F. Olson, 1972

WINTER SONGSTER

The voices of most song-birds, however joyous, suffer a long winter eclipse; but the Ouzel sings on through all the seasons and every kind of storm. However dark and boisterous the weather, snowing, blowing, or cloudy, all the same he sings, and with never a note of sadness. No need of spring sunshine to thaw *his* song, for it never freezes. Never shall you hear anything wintry from *his* warm breast; no pinched cheeping, no wavering notes between sorrow and joy; his mellow, fluty voice is ever tuned to downright gladness, as free from dejection as cock-crowing.

It is pitiful to see wee frost-pinched sparrows on cold mornings in the mountain groves shaking the snow from their feathers, and hopping about as if anxious to be cheery, then hastening back to their hidings out of the wind, puffing out their breast-feathers over their toes, and subsiding among the leaves, cold and breakfastless, while the snow continues to fall, and there is no sign of clearing. But the Ouzel never calls forth a single touch of pity; not because he is strong to endure, but rather because he seems to live a charmed life beyond the reach of every influence that makes endurance necessary.

One wild winter morning, when Yosemite Valley was swept its length from west to east by a cordial snow-storm, I sallied forth to see what I might learn and enjoy. A sort of gray, gloaming-like darkness filled the valley, the huge walls were out of sight, all ordinary sounds were smothered, and even the loudest booming of the falls was at times buried beneath the roar of the heavy-laden blast. The loose snow was already over five feet deep on the meadows, making extended walks impossible without the aid of snow-shoes. I found no great difficulty, however, in making my way to a certain ripple on the river where one of my ouzels lived. He was at home, busily gleaning his breakfast among the pebbles of a shallow portion of the margin, apparently unaware of anything extraordinary in the weather. Presently he flew out to a stone against which the icy current was beating, and turning his back to the wind, sang as delightfully as a lark in springtime.

—*John Muir, 1894*

An ouzel flies through an icy waterfall to reach its home, by Jeff Foott.

CHRISTMAS-TREE NEST

It was fairly late in the afternoon of December 23 when Sean, as the oldest boy, brought the tree home. They had gone out to Hanover County, he and a close friend, to a place where they "had permission," and there they had engaged in a long, judicious search through the cold and quiet woods. They had thought about bringing home a yearling pine, as a novelty, and had abandoned that idea as too much of a novelty; and finally, after two or three spruces had failed of confirmation for want of a unanimous vote, they had come across a cedar that seemed the perfect cedar.

It was in a little grove of cedars, halfway up a north slope above the stream where the two of them fished in summers, and it had the look and the shape and the air of a Christmas tree. So they felled it with an ax (a saw would have been neater, but a hundred years of custom decree that the tree must be *chopped* down, not *sawed* down), and they had dragged it down the snowy slope and across the frozen stream, stopping to inspect the thickness of the ice, which required some stomping and perilous leaping, and this had been followed by learned speculation on whether certain tracks were fox tracks or only dog tracks; but at last they had wrestled the tree into the back of a station wagon, complaining bitterly at the prickling of the needles, and what with one thing and another it was fairly late when the oldest boy brought the tree home.

Mounted in the living room, after appropriate sawing to make it stand forest straight again, the cedar seemed even larger than it had seemed in

the woods, there on the slope above the stream, so that some pruning and shaping had to be done; and the middle-sized boy (this was Chris, at eleven) had to learn for himself that if you seize a cedar too firmly, you *will* get stuck; and it is not yet time, he had to be told sixteen times, to put on the tinsel; and yes, he could hang on some ornaments after the angel was made secure on top.

It was at this moment that the littlest boy (son Kevin, at eight) made the discovery.

"Look!" he cried, and his voice held pure wonder and delight. "There's a bird's nest!"

And so it was. Buried deep in the branches, unnoticed in the shadows of the woods, the nest had survived snow and ice, and chopping and stomping and leaping, and being dragged and transported, and pruning and shaping, and here it was in the living room, as serenely perfect as a nest could be—three inches across and about two inches deep, formed entirely of pine tags, with small thin needles on the outside and some larger, twiggier pieces in the center; and suddenly this humble nest, in the midst of a great glitter of packages and lights and red and golden balls, made this Christmas tree quite the loveliest of all.

It might have been a towhee's nest, or a lark's, or a finch's or a sparrow's. Precedents and citations from an Audubon Guide proved not a great help. The littlest boy, taking a proprietary interest in the proceedings, decided the case for himself.

"It was *her* nest," he ruled, placing a stubby finger on Plate 47, and sounding out the syllables, "the in-di-go bunting's nest."

The ornithologists might have objected, but that was the nest in the cedar tree that Christmas Eve—a proud nest, occupied by an indigo bunting contrived of pipe cleaners and bright blue foil, with three blue beads where the eggs used to be, a brown cup nestled anew in green and silver branches hung with fragile scarlet fruit.

—*James J. Kilpatrick,* The Foxes' Union

A GUIDE TO BIRDS' NESTS IN WINTER

Nests Containing a Layer of Mud; Inside Diameter About Four Inches

Robin: Grass-lined, no leaves or sticks in the frame. *Woodthrush:* Lined with rootlets; leaves in the frame. *Common Grackle:* Grass-lined; with weed stalks or sticks in the frame.

— ❄ —

Large Bulky Nest with Twig and Bark Strip Frame; Thick Inner Lining of Dark Rootlets

Catbird, Mockingbird, Brown Thrasher: Brown thrasher nests are larger than the other two and contain foot-long or longer twigs. The catbird tends to put cellophane in its frame. *Cardinal:* Nest is lined with grasses instead of rootlets; no leaves in frame. These nests are most often found in shrubs, and are used by mice as winter homes.

Small Nests Neatly Formed of Grasses, Usually Lower Than Three Feet off the Ground

Song, Chipping, and Field Sparrows: All make small, neatly cupped grass nests, often placing them on the ground or a few feet off the ground. Some may be lined with horsehair or, in these days, nylon fishing line.

— ❄ —

Hanging Nests Suspended from Branch Tips

Northern Oriole: Grayish nests woven of yarn, plant fibers, hair, etc., often hanging from drooping branch tips of elms. Outside diameter about four inches.

Small, Neatly Formed Nests of Milkweed or Thistle Down and Grasses, Often in the Crotches of Sapling Trees

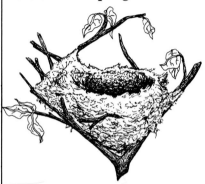

Redstart, Yellow Warbler, Goldfinch, Flycatchers: Downy materials show as gray or white in nest frame. Some have thick, sturdy walls. Weathering greatly alters these nests, making it difficult to identify them.

— ❄ —

Small Nests Neatly Suspended at their Rim to a Forking Branch

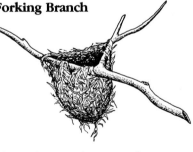

Vireos: Open at the top and built below the branch; outside diameter about three inches. The frame is woven with plant fibers and spider silk; lined with pine needles and fine grasses. Nests can be found at any height. More common in woods.

Adapted from *A Guide to Nature in Winter,* by Donald W. Stokes.

DECEMBER 24

YELLOWSTONE

"And, again, the coldest place in the nation last night was West Yellowstone, Montana." That's a song we've heard before, winter after winter on the nightly news, a kind of weatherperson's joke. It's all most American citizens know about Yellowstone in winter.

Yellowstone is a sacred place, believe it. And it is sacred for reasons beyond landscape and Old Faithful and even the great waterfall on the Yellowstone River. It is sacred for reasons that have nothing to do with our American pride in having at least tried to save some special part of that fresh green continent our people found and overwhelmed with our cities and automobiles and survey lines. It is mainly sacred because of the ecosystem that survives there.

After the tourists are gone Yellowstone belongs to nature again, to the forests and the fungi and, most visibly, to the great animals.

The snows begin to sift through the branches of the Douglas fir, and the interior of the park is officially shut down to automobile traffic.

Imagine forty below. It's colder than the temperature inside your freezer, and not uncommon when winter has come down on the park like the hammer it can be. The first heavy snows roll in from the Pacific in great waves, as though they might go on forever in some inexorable end-of-the-world scenario. The plateau around Yellow-

A buffalo herd forages in snowy Yellowstone National Park, by Steven Fuller.

142

After the tourists are gone, Yellowstone belongs to nature again,
to the forests and the fungi and, most visibly, to the great animals.

stone Lake is over 7,700 feet high, and the snow piles up five feet deep on the level. The heavy-browed bison plow along, swinging their heads to sweep away the snow and uncover buried yellow grass. The coyotes prey on tunneling rodents who have come up for air, make predatory moves toward buffalo calves, and study the otters at their fishing, hoping to frighten them away from their catch. It doesn't often work.

The cold is now sometimes terrible, and always there. Wind sculpts the frozen snow, and steam rises from the hot pools. The ice on Yellowstone Lake sings its music of tension, the coyotes answering back on clear nights. Elk wade in the Firehole, which is fed by hot springs, and feed on the aquatic life. This is winter in the high northern Rockies. Things have always been like this, except for the snowmobiles.

My friend Dave Smith, who was a winter keeper in Yellowstone for six years, says the park in winter is dappled with secret places.

"Living by yourself," he says, "you make a pact with trouble." Which sounds like a way of saying "death." Some simple mistake, like a bad fall on

Yellowstone's winter wonderland: encased in snow and ice, "ghost trees" (left) stand as white sentinels, by Frank S. Balthis; thermal steam billows along tourists' path (below), by Steven Fuller.

cross-country skis, can kill you very quickly when the daytime temperatures run to twenty below and night starts to come in out of the east at four in the afternoon.

"But once you've settled your mind," he says, "then you just go out there, and you find the warm places, where some little steam vent comes up from the thermal. The ground is soft, and green things are growing." Which is what he means, I guess, when he talks about secret places.

"Winter," Smith says, "is a time of dreams."

—*William Kittredge, 1984*

— ❄ —

The spectacular geothermal activity which gives Yellowstone its well-know geysers also helps some resident wildlife survive the harsh winters. Around hot pools and springs, rising steam melts some of the surrounding snow, uncovering food that would otherwise remain buried in Yellowstone's deep snow. Grass remains green around these pools in winter, providing succulent grazing for hungry elk and bison.

Overflow from hot springs also warms nearby rivers and keeps them from freezing. Moose and elk eat aquatic plants which thrive on the extra warmth, and trumpeter swans and Canada geese spend the winter in relative comfort there.

These unique conditions permit unusually large concentrations of animals near the thermal areas. But not all Yellowstone animals can take advantage of this limited resource, and for the rest, winter is still a rough time. Some, like the hardy bison and the long-legged moose, stick it out; others, like mule deer and many elk, migrate to lower, less snowy areas outside the park.

A hungry coyote eyes a river otter's catch (left), by Jerry L. Hill. A female elk comes to a free-flowing creek in search of food (below), by Steven C. Wilson.

THE ELK AND I

On a stormy Christmas Eve we drove slowly homeward over a lonely road after a last-minute shopping trip into Jackson, Wyoming. In a few hours, the whole community would be snow-bound. Sixteen inches of new snow had accumulated during the afternoon and, as dusk blended into darkness, more flakes were swirling into deepening drifts. A few miles beyond the edge of town, I began to wonder if we could make it.

I shifted into four-wheel drive. Windshield wipers groaned to keep twin triangles clear of snow. Then, as we rounded a bend, a phalanx of snow-plastered figures suddenly loomed ahead. I hit the brakes hard, the motor stalled and we slid to a stop. What we saw was incredible.

In single file, twenty-five splendid bull elk plodded across the road and plunged flank-deep into a steep snowbank toward the Gros Ventre River. They paid no attention to us. We could hear the crunch of hooves cracking brittle ice and splashing across the current long after the animals themselves had disappeared.

Over the years, my wife Peggy and I have seen a lot of wildlife around our scenic mountain home, but that elk encounter remains one of our most thrilling experiences. It was more than chance, too, because the annual migration of the elk out of the Teton Mountains down to their wintering ground in Jackson Hole was under way. "Those bulls," Peggy reflected, "seemed to be hurrying home for Christmas."

As autumn blends into winter, we watch the elk return to lower elevations. Deeper and deep-

er snows drive the herds farther and farther down. The bulls, fighting only recently, are friends again. They pass near our home on the same old trails they have always used. But they are skittish from the hunting seasons that have just closed and they tend to move mostly at night. We note their passage more from fresh tracks in the snow than from actual sightings. By Christmas, most of the elk in the Jackson-Teton-Yellowstone herds have safely reached the National Elk Refuge for the winter.

On another Christmas Eve we drove to the Grand Teton National Park, stepped into our cross-country skis and followed one of our favorite trails along the Snake River. It's always an exhilarating experience to be out skiing over snow

In winter, elk living in Wyoming's Teton Mountains descend to Jackson Hole: above, by Jon H. Jourdonnais; right, by J. Wright.

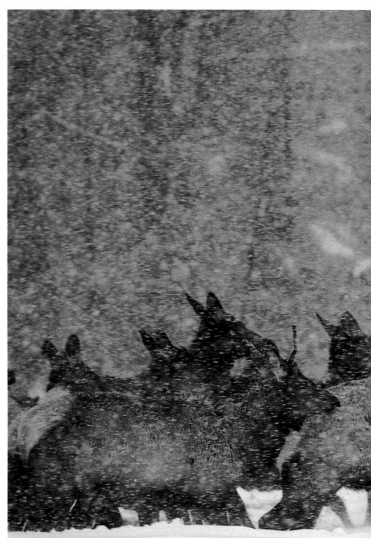

148

untracked by other people. Almost immediately, we were among hundreds of elk. Most of them seemed unafraid of us, moving only a short distance out of our path, then stopping to stare. A few that were bedded down didn't even bother to get up as we skied by. Although it turned bitterly cold toward dusk and frost crystals formed around our ski caps, we stayed out until almost totally dark. The December night was full of stars. The elk were ghostly shadows. Next morning, Christmas, it was snowing lightly. A single elk's tracks, made during the night, passed near our back door and aimed directly east toward the refuge.

—*Erwin A. Bauer, 1981*

Photographer Erwin A. Bauer stalks Wyoming elk on cross-country skis, by Peggy Bauer.

SHIVERING SHUTTERBUGS

❆ Nature in winter is probably one of the most breathtaking photographic subjects. However, cold weather poses special problems. Here are some tips which may help your winter photography trips.

❆ Camera parts can stiffen and may stop working altogether in frigid temperatures. Warm your camera before setting out, and snuggle it inside your parka when you are not shooting.

❆ Batteries can die suddenly in the bitter cold. If your camera or light meter uses batteries to operate, put a new battery in before your trip—and bring at least one spare.

❆ Cold film gets brittle and is easily torn. Advance and rewind the film gently and evenly. When you reach the end of the roll, stop advancing the film as soon as you feel any resistance. Keep spare rolls of film warm by carrying them next to your body.

❆ Frost can easily form on lenses from your breath. A lens shade helps, as well as breathing through your mouth and directing the air away from the camera.

❆ If you go into a warm, humid room or car after shooting outside, condensation could harm your equipment. Putting your camera in a plastic bag before going inside will protect your gear.

Condensed from "Photography Below Zero," by Keith Gunnar, *Backpacker* magazine, January 1984.

149

DECEMBER 25

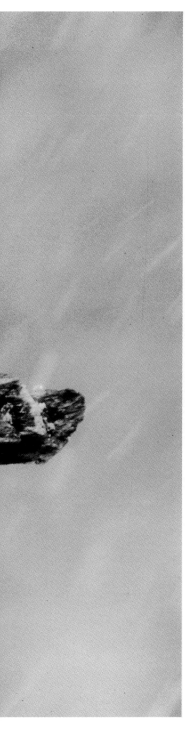

A pair of hardy Cassin's finches rests on a woody perch, by Erwin and Peggy Bauer.

THE SEQUOIA

Winter comes suddenly, arrayed in storms. You hear strange whisperings among the tree-tops, as if the giants were taking counsel together. One after another, nodding and swaying, calling and replying, spreads the news, until all with one accord break forth into glorious song, welcoming the first grand snowstorm of the year, and looming up in the dim clouds and snowdrifts like lighthouse towers in flying scud and spray. Studying the behavior of the giants from some friendly shelter, you will see that even in the glow of their wildest enthusiasm, when the storm roars loudest, they never lose their god-like composure, never toss their arms or bow or wave like the pines, but only slowly, solemnly nod and sway, standing erect, making no sign of strife, none of rest, neither in alliance nor at war with the winds, too calmly, unconsciously noble and strong to strive with or bid defiance to anything. Owing to the density of the leafy branchlets and great breadth of head the Big Tree carries a much heavier load of snow than any of its neighbors, and after a storm, when the sky clears, the laden trees are a glorious spectacle, worth any amount of cold camping to see. Every bossy limb and crown is solid white, and the immense height of the giants becomes visible as the eye travels the white steps of the colossal tower, each relieved by a mass of blue shadow.

In midwinter the forest depths are as fresh and pure as the crevasses and caves of glaciers. Grouse, nuthatches, a few woodpeckers, and other hardy birds dwell in the groves all winter, and the squirrels may be seen every clear day frisking about, tunneling to their stores, never coming up empty-mouthed, diving in the loose snow about as quickly as ducks in water, while storms and sunshine sing to each other.

—John Muir, 1901

*...his wanderings took him to the foot of an awesome sight:
the gigantic General Grant tree.*

— ❖ —

OUR NATIONAL CHRISTMAS TREE

The year was 1924 and the giant redwoods in California's Kings Canyon National Park were crowned with frozen tiaras from December's first snowfall. Charles Lee walked slowly beneath the towering trees, reflecting on the peacefulness of that High Sierra setting. Lee lived in the nearby town of Sanger, and he had visited the park many times. On this particular afternoon, his wanderings took him to the foot of an awesome sight: the gigantic General Grant tree. The huge redwood had been spreading its roots there for nearly 2,000 years—15 centuries before the first Europeans settled in the New World.

Staring up at the tree, Lee was unaware that a young girl had come up beside him. "What a wonderful Christmas tree that would be," she whispered, then ran off into the woods to join her family. Lee never forgot the youngster's words. Accompanied by some friends the following year, he returned to the site and held a short Yuletide service below the tree. "We all felt so good after that outing," he later recalled, "that I decided to do it every year." Lee's elation moved him to write the White House, suggesting that the General Grant be designated as the nation's "official" Christmas tree. Four months later, President Coolidge did just that.

Soaring 267 feet into the sky and measuring more than 100 feet around, the General Grant is one of the two largest living trees in the U.S. It is also among the oldest. Its age is surpassed in North America only by the ancient bristlecone pines that grow in eastern California, Nevada and Utah. Foresters estimate the Grant's weight at over 5,000 tons. Its 550,000 board feet of timber, they speculate, could supply enough wood to construct a 100-mile-long fence, or to build a crate to house the *Queen Mary*. Just one other tree of its kind, the 272-foot General Sherman in adjacent Sequoia National Park, is bigger.

Ever since Charles Lee conducted the first Yuletide service at the foot of General Grant, an annual ceremony has been held there on the second Sunday in December. The first official national celebration took place in 1926, shortly after President Coolidge's declaration. According to Park Service records, among those present at that celebration was a young man from Reedley, California, Peter Beier. Being "a man of regular habits," Beier is proud of the fact that he has attended every ceremony since. Now a hearty octogenarian with sparkling eyes, he recalls one service he almost missed.

In December of 1971, a fierce blizzard blasted the western slope of the High Sierra, making passage nearly impossible. So tough was the going that the residents of Sanger decided to hold their annual service in the foothills, eight miles outside of the park. Only Beier and some park rangers groped their way through the woodlands on snowshoes to lay the traditional wreath at the base of the tree. "Maybe it wasn't very prudent of me to go there," admits Beier, "but I guess I could be forgiven. I was a lot younger then." At that time, Beier was just 71.

—Jerry D. Lewis, 1981

Portrait of the National Christmas Tree: The General Grant sequoia stands tall in Kings Canyon National Park, California, by Joseph Muench.

DECEMBER 26

SNOWBOUND

Winter has its compensations. When snow comes to Rappahannock, country living takes on a new dimension. A Southerner embarks with diffidence upon tales of winter tribulations. A decent respect must be paid to those who have too much snow, or never quite enough. This is the way it is with mixed blessings. Poets may rhapsodize over honeysuckle and water hyacinths, but if you farm in the lowlands or live by the bayous, you rapidly lose enthusiasm for them. So it is with snow. A good part of the nation views a foot of fresh snow as Alabama views a field of fire ants. At the same time, one has to sorrow for those transplanted New Englanders, living in palmy exile in Miami or Fort Lauderdale, who hunger for the stuff that Minnesota would gladly give away.

Virginians never know quite what to make of snow. They are like barnyard geese. I read somewhere that a biologist once rated wild geese as having the greatest memories of any creatures known to science; barnyard geese, by contrast, evidently think the world begins anew each day. They cannot remember what happened yesterday afternoon. That is how it is with Virginians and snow. In Brainerd or Fargo or Butte, a couple of inches of snow can fall before breakfast, and nobody looks up from his flapjacks. The same snow in Virginia is a major event. The Richmond papers break out their 96-point Second Coming type: "Blizzard Paralyzes City." All the schools close; a thousand cars slide into a thousand other cars; we suffer something awful. Truth is, we ordinarily suffer mighty little.

The first flakes fell at 7 o'clock. Coming in from the woodpile, I felt the cold wet kiss of snow. In an instant, or so it seemed, the night had become a magic theater and the hemlocks a corps de ballet. A big spruce was hoopskirted and ruffled, a small pine in tutu. Yet the moment was caught on a soundless stage. Living in the city, we forget what silence is. In the whole of the night, only the snow was moving, falling, falling straight down, straight as lace curtains; sifting, clinging, obscuring the ruts of the red clay road. This was the way it was while Snow White slept, with the woods in ermine and the world enchanted.

At dawn the snow was falling still, and all the world was white on white, the fallen trees embossed upon the hill, the new stone wall a perfect parapet. The Rudasill's Mill Road had vanished as completely as if an illusionist had waved his wand. There was only a white cotton blanket spread in a split-rail crib. When at last the snow stopped, it left behind a wedding cake morning, the trees with pearl embroidered trains, edged in frosted lace. From the kitchen window, we could see only the birds in intermittent flight—red cardinals and blue juncos, titmice and grosbeaks, a ragged band of urchin sparrows.

All that morning the radio crackled of meetings cancelled, of schools closed, of speeches postponed, of stores and factories shutting down.

Abruptly the thought struck home: We were snowed in. Ordinarily any one of three roads will take us out to what, provisionally, may be styled as civilization. You can go south to Woodville, or north to Sperryville, or east by way of the Shade Road and come out on Route 211 just past the high school. We telephoned around the neighborhood. It would be pointless, it appeared, even to try to clear the driveway, for the Woodville road was blocked by 12-foot drifts on down by Clifton Clark's place. The Sperryville road was blocked at Jim Bill Fletcher's. And the Shade Road was impassable also.

Snow veils an old mill in New Jersey, by Breck P. Kent.

A snowstorm smothers a New England farm (right), by Clyde H. Smith. Along an unplowed road in Vermont, a fence (opposite) stands buried after a storm, by Roger Archibald.

These advisories produced a twinge of panic, and the mind probes at panic like a tongue at a toothache. If there were a fire, the volunteers couldn't get through. If there were a serious accident—a heart attack, a broken bone—no rescue squad could be summoned. Eventually, we figured, someone would come to dig us out. Jimmy Falls would plow around the Woodville drift, in order to get hay to his cattle. Mr. Manwaring would send Bob Grigsby to rediscover the driveway. Highway crews in time would do the rest. Meanwhile, we were prisoners.

Then a second thought struck home: Accept it. The thought has recurred many times since. In the sum total of man's brief span upon the earth, what would be missed? Truly missed? So the choirboys would not rehearse, nor the Kiwanians convene that day, and the schoolboys of Culpeper would miss the conjugation of their verbs. For the time being, there could be no further work upon the new stone wall; but the wall could wait. Somewhere a local court had closed; but justice would be done tomorrow, or the day after, or next week.

It is no bad thing, for a while at least, to find oneself snowbound. In his poignant novel of World War I, *The Fountain,* Charles Morgan put this feeling of cessation into words. In winter, he wrote, time stands still; nothing changes so long as snow is on the ground. And when time stands still, there is time for those things one never has time for otherwise. There are books to be read, and nuts to be cracked, and stamps to be put in philatelic albums. Most especially, there is time to talk. We do so little of that these days, for there are always Things That Have To Be Done; there are always appointments that must be kept, and deadlines that must be met. We get absorbed in the getting and spending.

Snowbound, it is possible to get absorbed in the things that count, in the giving and sharing of love that glows with a steady lantern's light, in the easy communion of books and conversation. There is a certain freedom in captivity, a certain

*Snowbound, it is possible to get absorbed in the things that count, . . .
in the easy communion of books and conversation.*

— ❄ —

peacefulness in being prisoner. In the mountains, the absolute obligations come down to very few—to feed the animals, to keep the fires going, to look after the elementary necessities of existence. It is wonderful to discover how many things, without calamity, can be postponed. Too soon the snowplow comes, a great orange beetle, grossly beaked, grinding a path by which schoolboys and choirs and Kiwanians can meet again. We learn from snowbound days.

All this is wrapped up in "country living." Nothing much happens up here in the Blue Ridge Mountains—only life, birth, death, law, philosophy, the harvest of a summer, the etched impression of a snowy night.

—James J. Kilpatrick, The Foxes' Union

THE SNOW-STORM

*Announced by all the trumpets of the sky,
Arrives the snow, and, driving o'er the fields,
Seems nowhere to alight: the whited air
Hides hills and woods, the river, and the heaven,
And veils the farm-house at the garden's end.
The sled and traveler stopped, the courier's feet
Delayed, all friends shut out, the housemates sit
Around the radiant fireplace, enclosed
In a tumultuous privacy of storm.*

—Ralph Waldo Emerson, 1847

DECEMBER 27

A COUGAR'S ROMP

After a heavy snowfall, one December morning, I started on skis for two weeks' camping in the Colorado Rockies. The fluffy snow lay smooth and unbroken over the broken mountains. Here and there black pine and spruce trees uplifted arrow-heads and snow-cones of the white mantle.

For an hour I followed a stream whose swift waters splashed up through the broken, icy skylights. Then leaving the cañon and skirting the slope, I was on the plateau summit of the Continental Divide, twelve thousand feet above the sea.

This summit moor was deeply overlaid with undrifted snow. Southward it extended mile after mile, rising higher and higher into the sky in broken, snow-covered peaks. To the north the few small broken cliffs and low buttes emphasized the trackless solitude. This plateau or moorland was less than one mile wide and comparatively smooth. Its edges descended precipitously two thousand feet into cirques and cañons.

Southward I travelled along the nearly level expanse of undrifted snow. Looking back along the line of my ski tracks, I saw a mountain lion leisurely cross from east to west. Apparently she had come up out of the woods for mad play and slaughter among the unfortunate snowbound folk of the summit. She stopped at my tracks for an interested look, turned her head, and glanced back along the way I had come. Then her eyes appeared to follow my tracks to the boulder pile from behind which I was then looking.

In Colorado, a cougar wanders past a stream, by Ernest Wilkinson.

Playfully bouncing off the snow, she struck into my ski prints with one forepaw, lightly as a kitten. Then she dived into them, pretended to pick up something between her forepaws, reared, and with a swing tossed it into the air. Then her playful mood changed and she started on across the Divide. After several steps she stopped, looking back as if she had forgotten something but was a little too lazy to retrace her steps. But finally she came back. She walked along my tracks for a few steps, then began to romp, now and then making a great leap forward, and rolled and struck about with the pretence of worrying something she had captured. She repeated this pantomime a few times, and then, as if suddenly remembering her original plan, again walked westward. Arriving at the summit she hesitated, and when I saw her last she was calmly surveying the scenes far below.

—*Enos Mills, 1920*

THE EYES OF A MOUNTAIN LION

I stepped closer and put my face within six inches of the lion's. He promptly spat on me. I had to steel my nerve to keep so close. But I wanted to see a wild lion's eyes at close range. They were exquisitely beautiful, their physical properties as wonderful as their expression. Great half globes of tawny amber, streaked with delicate wavy lines of black, surrounding pupils of intense purple fire. Pictures shone and faded in the amber light—the shaggy tipped plateau, the dark pines and smoky canyons, the great dotted downward slopes, the yellow cliffs and crags. Deep in those live pupils, changing, quickening with a thousand vibrations, quivered the soul of this savage beast, the wildest of all wild Nature, unquenchable love of life and freedom, flame of defiance.

—*Zane Grey, 1924*

THE WILD SHEEP

When the winter storms set in, loading their highland pastures with snow, then, like the birds, the wild sheep gather and go to lower climates, usually descending the eastern flank of the range to the rough, volcanic table-lands and treeless ranges of the Great Basin adjacent to the Sierra.

*. . . a small band of wild sheep had weathered the storm
in the lee of a clump of Dwarf Pines . . . .*

They never make haste, however, and seem to have no dread of storms, many of the strongest only going down leisurely to bare, wind-swept ridges, to feed on bushes and dry bunch-grass, and then returning up into the snow. Once I was snow-bound on Mount Shasta for three days, a little below the timber line. It was a dark and stormy time, well calculated to test the skill and endurance of mountaineers. The snow-laden gale drove on night and day in hissing, blinding floods, and when at length it began to abate, I found that a small band of wild sheep had weathered the storm in the lee of a clump of Dwarf Pines a few yards above my storm-nest, where the snow was eight or ten feet deep. I was warm back of a rock, with blankets, bread, and fire. My brave companions lay in the snow, without food, and with only the partial shelter of the short trees, yet they made no sign of suffering or faint-heartedness.

—John Muir, 1894

"Rocky Mountain Chase," oil painting by Guy Coheleach, 1979.

DECEMBER 28

ICE FISHING

You choose for this pastime a pond where the ice is not too thick, lest the labour of cutting through should be discouraging; nor too thin, lest the chance of breaking in should be embarrassing. You then chop out, with almost any kind of a hatchet or pick, a number of holes in the ice, making each one six or eight inches in diameter, and placing them about five or six feet apart. If you know the course of a current flowing through the pond, or the location of a shoal frequented by minnows, you will do well to keep near it. Over each hole you set a small contrivance called a "tilt-up." It consists of two sticks fastened in the middle, at right angles to each other. The stronger of the two is laid across the opening in the ice. The other is balanced above the aperture, with a baited hook and line attached to one end, while the other is adorned with a little flag. For choice, I would have the flags red. They look gayer, and I imagine they are more lucky.

When you have thus baited and set your tilt-ups,—twenty or thirty of them,—you may put on your skates and amuse yourself by gliding to and fro on the smooth surface of the ice while you wait for the pickerel to begin their part of the performance. They will let you know when they are ready.

A fish, swimming around in the dim depths under the ice, sees one of your baits, fancies it, and takes it in. The moment he tries to run away with it, he tilts the little red flag into the air and waves it backward and forward. "Be quick!" he signals all unconsciously; "here I am; come and pull me up!"

When two or three flags are fluttering at the same moment, far apart on the pond, you must skate with speed and haul in your lines promptly.

How hard it is, sometimes, to decide which one you will take first! That flag in the middle of the pond has been waving for at least a minute;

but the other, in the corner of the bay, is tilting up and down more violently: it must be a larger fish. Great Dragon! there's another red signal flying, away over by the point! You hesitate, you make a few strokes in one direction, then you whirl around and dart the other way. Meanwhile one of the tilt-ups, constructed with too short a cross-stick, has been pulled to one side, and disappears in the hole. One pickerel in the pond carries a flag. Another tilt-up ceases to move and falls flat upon the ice. The bait has been stolen. You dash desperately towards the third flag and pull in the only fish left,—probably the smallest of all!

A surplus of opportunities does not insure the best luck.

A room with seven doors—like the famous apartment in Washington's headquarters at Newburgh—is an invitation to bewilderment. I would rather see one fair opening in life than be confused by three dazzling chances.

—*Henry van Dyke, 1899*

— ❉ —

Apparently, not all ice-fishing experiences lend themselves to peaceful, long thoughts or breezy ice skating. Clifford B. Moore, in his book *Ways of Mammals in Fact and Fancy,* tells of this ice-fishing trip with an unexpected, startling finale.

Andrew J. Stone sat on the border of a lake one day, fishing through the ice. The winter day was cold and blustery, so Stone snuggled deep into his fur coat and turned up the collar high around his head. Suddenly, without warning, a powerful blow across his back sent him sprawling across the ice. Still stunned, he groped for his gun. As he turned on his assailant, he saw a mountain lion beating a hasty retreat toward the nearby woods. The bewildered cougar's dinner turned out to be nothing but an ice fisherman in fur clothing.

AMERICAN WINTER SPORTS.

"Trout Fishing 'on Chateaugay Lake'," Currier and Ives lithograph, 1856.

165

DARK HOUSE

It was just ten years ago that Bob came home to catch the feeling of the Minnesota-Ontario border country in midwinter. He wanted, above all, to sit in a dark house with me again and watch the circling decoy and the scene below the ice. He wanted time to think long thoughts and hear the whispering of the snow outside the thin tarpaper walls. He wanted the good feeling that he used to know at night after a long day on skis and perhaps the taste of a fish fresh from the icy waters of the lakes of the north.

So one morning, though it was twenty below, we took off for the old haunts. The ski harnesses creaked as we pushed across the lower reaches of Fall Lake. Smoke rose straight above the chimneys in the little town of Winton at the end of the road and the sun dogs blazed over the horizon. It was far too cold to travel slowly. We pushed hard on our sticks, and the skis hissed over the powder-dry snow. We were the only ones abroad, the only ones foolish enough to be outside when we did not have to be. Still, fresh deer tracks crossed the lake, and on the portage into Cedar there were signs of rabbits, weasels, and mice.

A tiny tarpaper shack off the end of a long point was our goal. A friend had set it up weeks ago, told us where the spear was cached and the wooden decoy. We shoveled the snow away from the door, fanned a flame to life in the little stove, and dug the spear and the decoy out of a drift.

Six inches of ice had to be cut out of the hole. We filled the coffeepot, closed the door, and settled down to wait. Outside the wind howled, but the little shelter was cozy and warm. At first we could see nothing but the green translucent water, but gradually our vision cleared and we could see farther and farther into the depths, finally to the very bottom itself. Light streamed through the snow and ice, and the bottom all but glowed.

In our field of vision were several whitish

rocks and bits of shell, important landmarks of the scene. Soon eel grass and feathery milfoil emerged in the half-light, weaving slowly in the slight current of the narrows. The rocks and shells became as familiar as though we had been watching them for weeks, the tufts of waving grass as outstanding as trees in a meadow.

I played the decoy, a six-inch model of a sucker minnow with fins and tail of shining tin. Whittled from a piece of cedar, it was weighted with lead and hung from the end of a string. Its tail was set so that with each motion of my hand it made wide and beautiful circles all around the hole.

After an hour of tension we began to relax, talked quietly about many things. A fish house is a fine place for visiting—not for arguments or weighty ideas, but rather for small talk, local politics and gossip, things we had seen coming in, ideas that required no effort, short simple thoughts that came as easily as breathing. This was no place for the expounding of strong, heady beliefs; such ideas need room and space in which to grow and expand. Furthermore, our energies must be conserved for the moment when the flash of a silver side below would eclipse everything else in the world.

The small talk went on and on, and after a while there was nothing more to say and we lapsed into quiet, just sat and stared into the hole, watching the rhythmic turns of the little decoy, back and forth, around and around, its metal fins flashing in the light. After a time our vision blended with the bottom itself and we began to feel as though we were a part of the subterranean world below us, part of the clean sand, the white rocks, the waving eel grass. We became intimately familiar with each irregularity of the bottom, the ripple marks, the moving habits of each blade of grass, the air bubbles at the edge of the ice, even the shadows of clouds drifting by outside. Two hours went by and our senses all but fused with the blue-green environment below.

Ice crystals in the upper atmosphere refract light from the sun, creating a pair of mock suns, called "sun dogs," by Jim Brandenburg.

Then when we had begun to feel as though nothing could ever change, as though we might have been sitting in that same position for years, a gray torpedo-like shape slipped swiftly into the open and the static little world we had created exploded. The grasses waved erratically, the white rocks disappeared, the water roiled.

The spear! screamed everything within us. Slowly—so slowly—cramped senses became aware, muscles began to move. As in a dream, fingers tightened around the cold, heavy steel; the point, withdrawn from its icy notch, hung poised, ready to strike. Directly below lay the gray shape of a great northern pike, its fins and tail moving slowly, its gill covers opening and closing with barely perceptible motion.

"Now!" came the shout, and suddenly the spear plunged, and in a violent instant the water boiled and the fish, the rocks, and the weeds disappeared in a green-white turmoil of confusion.

The spear and the fish came out of the hole in a cascade of water. I pushed out the door and we stumbled outside into the brilliant dazzle of sunlight on the snow, shouting, laughing at our good fortune, pounding each other on the back. This was a pinnacle of experience, and during that instant it seemed that few triumphs in the world of men could compare with it.

—*Sigurd F. Olson, 1957*

— ❄ —

To survive the nearly freezing lake water under the ice, many fish become dormant. They bury themselves in the mud or sit almost motionless on the bottom, using very little oxygen—the fish equivalent of hibernation in mammals. But predatory fish like great northern pike, pickerel, and muskellunge remain active, making easy meals of their sluggish neighbors. Swimming in the fast lane, however, may put these predators in the target range of an avid ice fisherman.

North American Indians supplemented their winter diets with fish caught through the ice. They speared large muskellunge, bass, lake trout, pike, and pickerel with 40-foot poles. Today, according to U.S. Fish and Wildlife Service figures, more than two million people ice fish.

White Bear Lake, near St. Paul, Minnesota, holds an annual ice fishing contest that draws four to five thousand anglers. And on many North American lakes, temporary ice fishing towns flourish as soon as the ice thickens. "Perchville," a shanty town on the Tawas Bay of Michigan's Lake Huron, even had its own mayor presiding at the intersection of Perch Street and Pike Avenue.

ICE FISHING TIPS

❀ The best ice fishing line is an old, stiff flycasting line. It runs freely and won't freeze, tangle, or collect snow out of water.

❀ To prevent the fishing hole from freezing, pour glycerine or cooking oil into it. The thin film over the water will keep ice from forming for a while.

❀ In winter, sluggish fish bite more delicately; use a light rod that responds easily to the gentle bites.

❀ Make sure the ice is thick enough to support your weight. A minimum of four inches is needed to support a man.

❀ In winter, use a small hook and small bait.

Tip-up and auger for ice fishing

Bait Suggestions

❀ Meal worms: inch-long beetle larvae found in damp, stored grain.

❀ June bugs: white larvae of June bug living in piles of decaying sawdust.

❀ Goldenrod galls: white grubs found in knobs on dry goldenrod stalks. Choose knob without holes, cut it open, and remove white grubs inside.

❀ Corn borers: small white worms found in cornstalks left in fields.

Adapted from *Country Scrapbook,* by Jerry Mack Johnson

Baked Stuffed Great Northern Pike

5-6-lb. pike
stuffing
6 strips of bacon or salt pork equivalent
1 small onion, finely chopped
4 tbsp. butter, melted
¼ cup white wine
watercress
lemon slices

Fill the dressed and scaled pike with the stuffing and sew up the opening (or use small skewers).

In a shallow baking dish or pan lay down a base of bacon strips and place the fish upon them, fastening with toothpicks. Fasten 2-3 strips of bacon or salt pork on top of the fish. Sprinkle with finely chopped onion.

Melt the butter, stir in the wine and keep warm.

Bake the fish in a 325° oven for 30-40 minutes, depending on size, but be sure to baste often with the butter and wine.

Garnish with watercress and lemon slices.

NOTE: If you wish, add oysters, canned shrimp, or canned minced clams to your own favorite sage and bread stuffing. Serves 6.

Pickerel and Potatoes

2 pickerel, scaled or skinned
6 potatoes, sliced thin
salt and pepper
6 cloves garlic, finely minced
6 tbsp. butter, melted
½ cup white wine
juice of 1 lemon
2 tbsp. chopped parsley

Lay the fish in a lidded casserole and arrange the potato slices over them.

Salt and pepper over all, then add the garlic and the melted butter.

Pour in the wine, then add enough water to come up to the potatoes. Cover, and cook over a low flame until the liquid is almost gone and potatoes are cooked—about 20 minutes.

Squeeze in the lemon, then sprinkle the parsley over all. Serves 4-6.

Adapted from *The L.L. Bean Game and Fish Cookbook,* by Angus Cameron and Judith Jones

DECEMBER 29

THE ICE HOWL

Winter was the testing time, the hard time of relentless cold, keening winds, and silent, endless snow.

It was a world new to the ear as well as to the eye. All the small sounds—the crackle of undergrowth, the fall of a pine cone, the whispering of a brook—were silenced. In the great stillness, the roar of the rapids was deeper, and the snapping of an overloaded branch louder and sharper. Human voices took on a clear, bell-like quality in the crystal air, and the bark of a fox in the distance sounded near and strangely sweet. There were no familiar echoes. Sounds did not reverberate as usual, but drifted on to become absorbed in the engulfing softness. It was odd and a little unsettling, as though the natural laws were suspended and the world slightly askew.

Most unsettling of all was the howl of the ice on the lakes in the windless silence. As it froze thicker and thicker, two, four, seven feet, it rifted under the increasing pressure. The crack would run the entire length or breadth of a lake, sometimes for several miles, accompanied by the sound of the faulting, a tremendous, half-human howl. It was blood-chilling to hear in the middle of the night, crying despairingly through the mountains and up to the moon. It was even more eerie in the daytime to stand on the shore of a frozen lake and hear the howling. Nothing moved on the candid, glittering expanse, not even a wreath of blown snow. And yet the howling came, starting faintly in the distance, increasing in volume as it approached, rising to a high shriek as it passed within feet of where you were standing, and fading as it retreated, wild and lost, to the far shore. It was like being brushed by a ghostly pack of invisible werewolves.

—Louise Dickinson Rich, 1962

Sunset on an Adirondack lake, by Bruce D. Thomas.

I HEARD A BIRD SING

I heard a bird sing
    In the dark of December
A magical thing
    And sweet to remember.

"We are nearer to Spring
    Than we were in September,"
I heard a bird sing
    In the dark of December.

       —Oliver Herford, c. 1915

*Fluffed up against the winter
chill, a meadowlark rests on a
snow-capped coneflower (left);
A flock of Canada geese takes
off from a marsh (below), both
by Gary R. Zahm.*

WINTER SOUNDS

For sounds in winter nights, and often in winter days, I heard the forlorn but melodious note of a hooting owl indefinitely far; such a sound as the frozen earth would yield if struck with a suitable plectrum, the very *lingua vernacula* of Walden Wood, and quite familiar to me at last, though I never saw the bird while it was making it. I seldom opened my door in a winter evening without hearing it; *Hoo hoo hoo, hoorer hoo,* sounded sonorously, and the first three syllables accented somewhat like *how der do;* or sometimes *hoo hoo* only. One night in the beginning of winter, before the pond froze over, about nine o'clock, I was startled by the loud honking of a goose, and, stepping to the door, heard the sound of their wings like a tempest in the woods as they flew low over my house. They passed over the pond toward Fair Haven, seemingly deterred from settling by my light, their commodore honking all the while with a regular beat. Suddenly an unmistakable cat-owl from very near me, with the most harsh and tremendous voice I ever heard from any inhabitant of the woods, responded at regular intervals to the

goose, as if determined to expose and disgrace this intruder from Hudson's Bay by exhibiting a greater compass and volume of voice in a native, and *boo-hoo* him out of Concord horizon. What do you mean by alarming the citadel at this time of night consecrated to me? Do you think I am ever caught napping at such an hour, and that I have not got lungs and a larynx as well as yourself? *Boo-hoo, boo-hoo, boo-hoo!* It was one of the most thrilling discords I ever heard. And yet, if you had a discriminating ear, there were in it the elements of a concord such as these plains never saw nor heard.

—*Henry David Thoreau, 1854*

— ❄ —

In crisp winter weather, sounds can carry astounding distances. When extremely cold, dry air near the ground is topped by warmer, moister air, sound travels along the earth's surface instead of dissipating into the atmosphere. At -60°F, for example, you may be able to hear dogs barking miles away.

"Rent Free," acrylic and casein painting by Guy Coheleach, 1974.

175

DECEMBER 30

ICE-STORM MAGIC

I reverently believe that the Maker who made us all makes everything in New England but the weather. I don't know who makes that, but I think it must be raw apprentices in the weather-clerk's factory who experiment and learn how, in New England, for board and clothes, and then are promoted to make weather for countries that require a good article, and will take their custom elsewhere if they don't get it. There is a sumptuous variety about the New England weather that compels the stranger's admiration—and regret. The weather is always doing something there; always attending strictly to business; always getting up new designs and trying them on the people to see how they will go.

Yes, one of the brightest gems in the New England weather is the dazzling uncertainty of it. There is only one thing certain about it: you are certain there is going to be plenty of it—a perfect grand review; but you never can tell which end of the procession is going to move first.

But, after all, there is at least one or two things about that weather (or, if you please, effects produced by it) which we residents would not like to part with. If we hadn't our bewitching autumn foliage, we should still have to credit the weather with one feature which compensates for all its bullying vagaries—the ice-storm: when a leafless tree is clothed with ice from the bottom to the top—ice that is as bright and clear as crystal; when every bough and twig is strung with ice-beads, frozen dew-drops, and the whole tree sparkles cold and white, like the Shah of Persia's diamond plume. Then the wind waves the branches and the sun comes out and turns all

After a North Carolina storm, a tree stands adorned with ice jewels, by Jack Dermid.

*. . . every bough and twig is strung with ice-beads, . . . and the whole
tree sparkles . . . like the Shah of Persia's diamond plume.*

— ❄ —

those myriads of beads and drops to prisms that
glow and burn and flash with all manner of colored fires, which change and change again with
inconceivable rapidity from blue to red, from red
to green, and green to gold—the tree becomes a
spraying fountain, a very explosion of dazzling
jewels; and it stands there the acme, the climax,
the supremest possibility in art or nature, of
bewildering, intoxicating, intolerable magnifi-
cence. One cannot make the words too strong.

—Mark Twain, 1876

*Icicles hang on a maple leaf
(above), by John Shaw. A
cardinal perches on an icy
tree (opposite), by Larry West.*

DEEP FREEZE

As usual, it started with a mid-winter thaw and
a cold, misty rain which coincided with steadily
dropping temperatures. The liquid film froze
upon contact, hence every branch and twig built
its own armor of clear ice.

Long before dawn a cold front had pushed that
storm out over the Atlantic. By sun-up our north
country was immersed in an elemental deep-
freeze. No outdoorsman can afford to sleep on the
first morning of an ice storm.

The existing snow cover offered no problem:
it was light and glazed with ice. Before I'd
donned heavy woolens and rubber-bottomed
shoe-pacs for a journey of reconnaissance, my
brother, Dick, discovered a ruffed grouse under
an apple tree at the end of our lawn.

The grouse was all fluffed up, insulated against
the cold. As big as a football, it strutted beneath
the tree, picked at infinitesimal weed seeds and
finally meandered into a grotesque jungle of
ice-coated brush.

Until the wind rises, such a jungle is a mixture
of incomparable beauty and Alice-in-Wonderland
vistas. Diamonds may be a girl's best friends, but
no courtesan ever witnessed jewelry to match that
strung on every twig during the first hours of a
true silver thaw.

A deep-freeze is silent, so you must go shortly
after dawn on a first day to appreciate a country-
side completely imprisoned and fixed at a moment
of struggle. It's a brittle world's end—truly
magnificent—and bearable only because you know
it can't last.

178

Entranced, I battered through a lacy wilderness of fine spun glass. Shards of ice chattered as they fell. There were no birds, no bouncing cottontails, no sign of the multitudinous life I knew existed in this wood.

They were there, of course—everything from the chickadee roosting in a conifer to the deer bedded in a thicket. They could afford to wait for Nature to loosen her iron grip. Wild creatures are programmed to such periods of chill and famine. The northern birds and mammals have known ice storms for a million years. Only mankind frets.

By 10 a.m. the breeze had freshened. Now our woodlands were a clattering bedlam of sound, of tortured tree trunks and branches recovering their positions after the ice had cracked, shattered and gone plummeting to earth.

By this time the grouse would be feasting, carefully gleaning the fat, male buds of aspen and ignoring the less nutritional female buds. Chickadees would be picking minuscule grubs from unburdened branches, and deer would be ghosting through the thickets, nibbling shoots of red maple and wild raspberry. The storm was, after all, just one of those things. It was part and parcel of northern wintertime, an event to suffer, to wait out, to enjoy—rarely a tragedy.

Unless, of course, the human intellect counts thousands of dead limbs brought to earth, plus the pruning of poorly grown live limbs a sorrow. Unless, as a human, you honestly dislike the classic, ice-induced curve of white birches.

—*Frank Woolner, 1972*

DECEMBER 31

A CHRISTMAS GOOSE

The phone call came late in the afternoon on the Sunday before Christmas. A couple of guys, fishing at a local reservoir, had found an injured bird. Could they bring it by the museum for care by our Wildlife Rescue Team? Sure, I told them.

My fourteen-year-old daughter and I had to drive down to the museum anyway. That's where my wife's presents were stashed; Corey was going along to help wrap them.

Two young men were waiting in front of the museum. The bird was wrapped in a towel, but the head and neck were uncovered; two bright black eyes quietly observed our every move.

It was an enormous Canada goose, one of those great grey and black honkers that wander across our crisp winter skies in endlessly searching Vs.

As she lay on the counter, her eyes were even with mine. The problem quickly became apparent.

Wound around the base of her neck was a heavy tangle of fishing line. She'd obviously not realized it when she'd become ensnared, and had kept right on eating until her esophagus above the cord had become swollen with food.

Now she was weak. So weak that she couldn't fly or even stand. She could only sit, with her three-foot wings folded silently along her back.

Cutting away the cord was the easy part. Clearing out the packed food without causing further injury was going to be the problem.

While Corey stood by our goose, I phoned the museum's veterinarian at home and filled him in. "A Christmas Goose?" he chuckled. "It figures!"

The choice was harshly simple. It was an emergency, and the procedure would be to make a small slit in the neck and physically remove the material. It was Sunday. Precious time would be lost if the vet drove to his hospital. So I thanked him over the phone for his advice. He wished us all the best of luck.

I looked at my daughter. "Ever read about Florence Nightingale?" I said. Her eyes darted to the goose's, then back to mine. She nodded.

Corey held the goose by both wings; the bird was suddenly so weak that her head sagged limply to the sink bottom. Her eyes started to close. No time to waste from here on.

Halfway through I glanced sideways at my daughter. Her face was white but her hands were still holding tight to the great bird's silent wings.

Finally, after several acorns, a bay seed the size of a large marble, and a last pungent pinch of water weed, we were through. We put a clean bandage around the goose's neck like a bit of white silk ribbon around a special Christmas package. With Corey still holding the bird, I quickly gave our feathered patient a cool, life-bringing draft of food and water.

By the time we three got home, that all-knowing head was again perched atop the sturdy neck, those sparkling black eyes were again meeting ours, matching each concerned glance with an equal gleam of confidence.

And would you believe what my wife and son were doing when we arrived? They were watching "The Miracle on 34th Street" on TV—that wonderful old classic about the department store Santa who claims to be the genuine Kris Kringle.

And so it came to pass that we named our

"Stretching—Canada Goose," acrylic painting by Robert Bateman, 1983.

Christmas Goose "Kris." And we cared for her in a special "gift-wrapped" box in the quiet corner behind the pile of Christmas packages by the tree. Her life was a priceless gift for us all.

Our family welcomed the New Year together by releasing our Christmas Goose at dawn on New Year's Day. Arm in arm we watched her disappear into the early morning sun.

And this Christmas, when children strain their ears for the jingle of sleighbells and the patter of tiny hooves on the roof, one family will listen for the faint honk of a high-flying Christmas Goose.

—*Gary L. Bogue, 1976*

A pair of Canada geese finds winter comfort (below), by C. W. Schwartz. A brown thrasher harvests a winter handout (right), by Tom J. Ulrich.

THURBER

Sometimes, either because of a bountiful food supply or because of an injury that kept it from migrating, a summer bird may remain with us all winter . . . .

[The winter of 1967] there was Thurber. We gave this name to a brown thrasher shortly after we'd discovered him huddled in our barn during the big Christmas snowstorm . . . . All his kind had left New England months before, and he was obviously some sort of holdover.

We brought Thurber into the house and turned him loose. There was nothing wrong with his flying ability that we could see, and he quickly took up residence in the little indoor garden in our bay window. There he gained strength on cranberries, raisins, and a few worms I found for him.

A brown thrasher is hardly an indoor bird, but we couldn't consign him to the bitter cold of midwinter, either. Something had to be done. But what? A friend of ours, a feature writer for a local newspaper, came to the rescue. Why not tell of Thurber's plight and see if the readers had any suggestions?

So, the next day, there was Thurber on page one. Did anybody have any ideas as to what to do with a bird you couldn't keep—and couldn't let go, either?

The story was hardly three hours old when our telephone rang. It was a lady from Burlington. She and her husband planned to jet down to Florida the next morning. If we could get Thurber to them they'd be glad to take him along. They could let him go when they landed.

We found a cat-carrying case made of heavy black cardboard. It would be perfect for the bird, as he'd remain quiet in its darkened interior. So

Mr. and Mrs. Jack Gladstone walked up that gangplank with two pieces of hand luggage: Mrs. Gladstone's pocketbook and Mr. Gladstone's "cat."

Three days later a post card showed up in our wind-swept mailbox. "Thurber went with the wind," it said. "And were all the passengers surprised when we got off the plane, opened the box, and let out a bird!"

In about a week the box was returned. Inside, we found a single slip of paper, with a sketch of a bird's foot and the single word: "Thanks." So for one bird that missed the boat, so to speak, all was not lost. He merely hopped a plane.

—Ronald Rood, 1973

O TANNENBAUM!

In January we'll have our Christmas tree up and decorated . . . again! Although the sparkling tinsel and twinkling lights will all be packed away in the attic, our Christmas tree will still stand, with a few alterations, of course.

For one thing, it will stand in the front yard rather than the front room. My husband drove a metal fence post into the ground before the earth froze, and the tree will be tied to that, providing a much needed extra windbreak on the west side of the bird feeder. Since we'll use a freshly-cut white pine when we ornament it indoors the first time, it will keep its color for several months outside.

This second decorating of the Christmas tree will be strictly for the birds, and the ornaments will vary according to available kitchen scraps. Often we adorn it with grapefruit halves, threading the empty rinds on heavy yarn and hanging them as yellow baskets from the pine boughs. We fill them with whatever is handy—crushed egg shells, hamburger grease, muffin crumbs. As time and full tummies allow, we may string some popcorn garlands. But we'll leave the colored light business to Mother Nature, who we hope will step in to add her own flashy baubles, the birds.

The juncos seem most fond of the temporary evergreen, nestling deep in its interior close to the trunk. A goldfinch doubles as a star, perched on the topmost point of the tree, surveying the feeder situation. He twirls around and around, checking out every direction before alighting on the ground to feed. Cardinals and purple finches pause within the needled shelter occasionally, their red and raspberry shining gaily against the green. Even the tree sparrows, with their rusty caps and black breast spots, will linger near the tree, although they prefer the ground beneath it.

Our recycled Christmas trees have been propped, tied, and leaned just about everywhere. One year the ground was too frozen to sink a support, so the tree was left on its side against the garage. The juncos flocked to it for protection from chilly night air and winds. Another year I had no real yard, so I lashed the tree to the railing of my back balcony. Orange halves stuffed with suet were the fare that season.

Sometime in mid-spring, when the tree begins to brown, we will drag it back to the brush pile along the edge of the field. There it will join its cousins from previous years, and together they will provide an impenetrable shelter for resting rabbits and roosting redbirds in winters to come.

—*Maryanne Newsom-Brighton, 1982*

Deck a tree for the birds: A pygmy nuthatch savors a digger pine cone with a peanut-butter frosting (above), by Kent and Donna Dannen; a female cardinal (right) feasts on an orange half, by Jen and Des Bartlett.

❄ In addition to stocking their feeders with a variety of seeds, more ambitious bird lovers can provide a gourmet menu for their feathered friends. Here are some easy-to-do recipes that will keep the birds coming to your yard.

Chickadee Pudding

The following recipe is a filler for hanging feeders made using aluminum pie plates, coconut shell halves, margarine tubs, or cardboard milk cartons with the tops cut off. To make the feeders, cut several holes (drill holes in coconut shells) and suspend the feeders with strong string.

1½ cup melted suet
2 tbsp. peanut butter
1 cup oatmeal
½ cup corn meal
1½ cup cereal crumbs
½ cup flour
¼ cup sugar or honey
2 cups bird seed

Mix all ingredients thoroughly, put into feeders. Set in cool place to harden before hanging outdoors.

Cornbread for the Birds

6 cups cornmeal
3 tsp. baking powder
⅔ cup shortening
6 cups water

Mix all ingredients thoroughly, pour into deep pan. Bake at 350° for about one half hour. When cool, break into pieces and scatter for the birds.

Peanut Ropes

Using a large needle and heavy thread or string, string together in any combination unshelled peanuts, popped popcorn, cranberries, raisins, apple pieces, and dried fruits. Hang the chains or wrap them around tree limbs.

Pine Cone Snacks

Mix together 1 cup peanut butter, ½ cup crumbs, and ½ cup finely chopped apple. Spread mixture in pine cone spaces. Tie string around the top of the cone first to suspend it.

Suet Stick

Find a dead branch about 2 to 3 inches thick and 16 inches long. Drill 1-inch-diameter holes in several places, but do not go through wood. Fasten a screw eye at one end. Press the suet into the holes and hang the branch from screw eye with a wire or coat hanger.

These and other recipes and ideas may be found in *A Complete Guide to Bird Feeding*, by John V. Dennis.

Nature looks ahead and makes ready for the new season in the midst of the old. The present season is always the mother of the next, and the inception takes place long before the sun loses its power.

—John Burroughs, 1905

A trumpeter swan in an icy Yellowstone river stretches its wings, by C. C. Lockwood.

TEXT CREDITS

Pages 162-163: "Rocky Mountain Chase," by Guy Coheleach, Bernardsville, NJ. **Page 165:** "American Winter Sports—Trout Fishing on Chateaugay Lake," by Currier and Ives, courtesy of the Museum of the City of New York. **Pages 174-175:** "Rent Free," by Guy Coheleach, Bernardsville, NJ. **Page 181:** "Stretching—Canada Goose," Robert Bateman artwork, courtesy of Mill Pond Press, Inc. From *The World of Robert Bateman,* a Random House-/Madison Press book, 1981.

Illustrations on **pages 21, 39, 71, 83, 97, 141,** and **169** by Robin Brickman.

We wish to thank the publishers, authors, or their representatives listed below for permission to reprint copyrighted material.

"December" (p. 6), condensation of "December Moon" (p. 36), and condensation of "The Ancients" (p. 78) from *Hal Borland's Twelve Moons of the Year,* edited by Barbara Dodge Borland, Alfred A. Knopf, Inc., 1979. Reprinted by permission of Barbara Dodge Borland. Copyright © 1979 by Barbara Dodge Borland.

"The House in Winter" (p. 9) is reprinted from *Collected Poems (1930-1973),* by May Sarton, with the permission of W. W. Norton & Company, Inc. Copyright © 1974 by May Sarton.

"Winter Neighbors" (p. 10) condensed from *Signs and Seasons,* by John Burroughs, Houghton, Mifflin & Co., Boston, 1886.

"Frost-work" (p. 12) reprinted from *The Poems of Thomas Bailey Aldrich,* Houghton, Mifflin & Co., Boston, 1882.

"Winter's Icy Lacework" (p. 14) and "Winter Sleepers" (p. 22) condensed from *An Almanac for Moderns,* by Donald Culross Peattie, G. P. Putnam's Sons, NY, 1935. Reprinted by permission of Noel R. Peattie and Curtis Brown Associates Ltd. Copyright © 1935, 1963 by Donald Culross Peattie.

"A Sharing of Persimmons" (pp. 16-19) and "When Clocks Go Wrong" (pp. 118-119) condensed from *Wildlings,* by Mary Leister. Copyright © 1976 by Mary Leister and reprinted from *Wildlings* by permission of Stemmer House Publishers, Inc., Owings Mills, MD.

Adapted recipes for "Persimmon Bread" and "Persimmon Cookies" (p. 21) reprinted from *Wild Fruits: An Illustrated Guide and Cookbook,* copyright © 1983 by Mildred Fielder. Used with permission of Contemporary Books, Inc., Chicago.

Recipe for "Persimmon Pudding" (p. 21) adapted from *Edible Wild Plants of Eastern North America,* by Merritt Lyndon Fernald and Alfred Charles Kinsey, revised by Reed C. Rollins. Copyright © 1958 by the President and Fellows of Harvard College. Reprinted by permission of Harper & Row, Publishers, Inc.

"A Snowdrift Den" (p. 24), "A Winter Muskrat" (p. 49), and "Thurber" (p. 183) are reprinted from *Who Wakes the Groundhog?* by Ronald Rood, by permission of W. W. Norton & Company, Inc. Copyright © 1973 by W. W. Norton & Company, Inc.

"Bears' Winter Music" (p. 24) from *The History of the American Indians,* by James Adair, London, 1775.

"Food for the Winter" (p. 24) from *The Natural History of North-Carolina,* by John Brickell, Dublin, 1737.

"The Woodpile" (p. 28) and "A Hillside Thaw" (p. 114) from *The Poetry of Robert Frost,* edited by Edward Connery Latham. Copyright 1923, 1930, 1939, © 1969 by Holt, Rinehart and Winston. Copyright 1951, © 1958 by Robert Frost. Copyright © 1967 by Lesley Frost Ballantine. Reprinted by permission of Holt, Rinehart and Winston, Publishers.

"Firewood Opportunists" (p. 30), "The Pine Woods" (p. 69), "Marshland Elegy" (p. 89), and "Warmth in Midwinter" (pp. 116-117) from *A Sand County Almanac, with Other Essays on Conservation from Round River,* by Aldo Leopold. Copyright © 1949, 1953, 1966, renewed 1977, 1981 by Oxford University Press, Inc. Reprinted by permission.

"Firelight Nights" (pp. 31-32), "The Starfield" (pp. 37-38), and "Lord of the Yard" (p. 123) condensed from *A Naturalist Buys an Old Farm,* by Edwin Way Teale. Reprinted by permission of the publisher, Dodd, Mead & Company, Inc. Copyright © 1974 by Edwin Way Teale.

Recipe for "Mulled Cider" (p. 33) reprinted with permission from *A Gift of Mistletoe,* compiled by Elizabeth Deane. Copyright © 1971 by Peter Pauper Press, Inc.

Condensed version of "What's a Three-Dog Night?" (p. 33) reprinted with permission from *The Cold Weather Catalog,* edited by Robert Levine and Nancy Bruning. Copyright © 1977 by Tree Communications, Inc.

"Moonlit Owl" (p. 34) and "An Arctic Visitor" (p. 122) condensed from *The Valley: Meadow, Grove and Stream,* by Lorus J. Milne and Margery Milne, Harper & Row, Publishers, Inc., NY, 1963. Copyright © 1959, 1963 by Lorus J. Milne and Margery Milne. Reprinted by permission of the authors.

"Legend of the Big Dipper" (p. 39) first published in *The Reporter,* 26 January 1967. Reprinted from *The Way to Rainy Mountain,* by N. Scott Momaday. Copyright © 1969, The University of New Mexico Press. Condensed version used by permission of The University of New Mexico Press.

TEXT CREDITS

Condensation of "My Fox" (pp. 40-42), and "Christmas Spruce" (p. 104) reprinted from *Wild Things,* by Dion Henderson, by permission of Wisconsin Trails/Tamarack Press. Copyright © 1979 by Dion Henderson.

"Call of the Fox" (pp. 42-43) reprinted from *Winter Sunshine,* by John Burroughs, Hurd & Houghton, NY, 1876.

"Red Fox Riviera" (p. 45) and "The Ever Hungry Jay" (pp. 100-103) condensed from *The Wildlife Stories of Faith McNulty,* Doubleday and Co., Inc., NY. Copyright © 1980 by Faith McNulty. Reprinted by permission of the author.

"Snow Meadow" (p. 46), condensation of "Winter Songster" (p. 138), and "The Wild Sheep" (pp. 161-163) from *The Mountains of California,* by John Muir, The Century Co., NY, 1894.

"The Snow" (p. 48) reprinted by permission of the publishers and the Trustees of Amherst College from *The Poems of Emily Dickinson,* edited by Thomas H. Johnson, Cambridge, MA: The Belknap Press of Harvard University Press. Copyright 1951, © 1955, 1979, 1983 by The President and Fellows of Harvard College.

First stanza of "Snow-flakes" (p. 50) from *Tales of a Wayside Inn,* by Henry Wadsworth Longfellow, Ticknor & Fields, Boston, 1863.

"A Blanket of Snow" (p. 52) from *A Cup of Sky,* by Donald Peattie and Noel Peattie. Copyright 1945, 1946, 1947, 1948, 1949, 1950 by Donald Culross Peattie. Copyright © renewed 1977 by Noel Peattie. Reprinted by permission of Houghton Mifflin Company.

"Timber Wolves" (pp. 55-56), "A Weasel's Trail" (p. 130), and "Dark House" (pp. 166-168) condensed by permission of Alfred A. Knopf, Inc. from *The Singing Wilderness,* by Sigurd F. Olson. Copyright © 1956 by Sigurd F. Olson.

"Built-in Snowshoes" (pp. 56-57) and "Resourceful Rabbit" (p. 74) from *Life-histories of Northern Animals,* by Ernest Thompson Seton, Charles Scribner's Sons, NY, 1909.

Condensation of "Winter in the Southwest" (p. 61), by Bob Schimmel, copyright © 1967 by the National Wildlife Federation. Reprinted from the December/January 1968 issue of *National Wildlife* Magazine.

"Stories in the Snow" (pp. 62-64) condensed from "How Wildlife Leaves Its Mark," by Anthony Acerrano, copyright © 1982 by the National Wildlife Federation. Reprinted from the October/November issue of *National Wildlife* Magazine.

"Reading Animal Signatures" (p. 65) and "A Guide to Birds' Nests in Winter" (p. 141) adapted from *A Guide to Nature in Winter,* by Donald W. Stokes. Copyright © 1976 by Donald W. Stokes. By permission of Little, Brown and Company.

"Adirondack Spruce" (p. 66), condensed from *Just About Everything in the Adirondacks,* by William Chapman White. Copyright © 1960 by The Adirondack Historical Association. Reprinted by permission of The Adirondack Museum. Grateful acknowledgment is made to the New York *Times* and the New York *Herald Tribune* for permission to reproduce columns from "Topics of the Times" and "Just About Everything."

"In the Aspen Grove" (p. 71) condensed from *Beyond the Aspen Grove,* by Ann Zwinger, Harper & Row, Publishers, Inc., NY. Reprinted by permission of the author. Copyright © 1981 by Ann Zwinger.

"Dancing Hares" (pp. 72-74) adapted from *Wintering,* by Diana Kappel-Smith. Copyright © 1979, 1980, 1982, 1984 by Diana Kappel-Smith. First appeared in *Blair and Ketchum's Country Journal.* By permission of Little, Brown and Company.

"Bruised Ego" (pp. 74-77) from *Bobcats Before Breakfast,* by John Kulish, Stackpole Books, Harrisburg, PA. Reprinted by permission of the author. Copyright © 1969 by John Kulish.

"The Lynx and the Hare" (p. 77) condensed from *A Naturalist in Alaska,* by Adolph Murie. Reprinted by permission of The Devin-Adair Company, Publishers. Copyright © 1961 by The Devin-Adair Company.

"Christmas" (p. 80) by Claire Mattern reprinted by permission from *Christmas with a Country Flavor* by the Editors of Farm Journal. Copyright © 1973, 1974, 1975 by Farm Journal, Inc.

Instructions for "Green Wreath" and "A Decorated Six-Pointed Star" (p. 83) are adapted from *The Gift of Christmas Past: A Return to Victorian Traditions,* by Sunny O'Neil. Copyright © 1981 by the American Association for State and Local History. Used by permission of the American Association of State and Local History.

"Tips for preserving your decorations ever green" (p. 83) adapted with permission from *Blair and Ketchum's Country Journal,* December 1983.

Condensation of "The Winter Marsh" (pp. 84-89), by Franklin Russell, reprinted by permission from *Audubon,* the magazine of the National Audubon Society, copyright 1969.

"Winter Animals" (pp. 92-94), "Barred Owl" (p. 120), and "Winter Sounds" (pp. 173-174) from *Walden,* by Henry David Thoreau, Ticknor & Fields, Boston, 1854.

"Feeder Dividends" (pp. 94-95) condensed from *In Praise of Seasons,* by Alan H. Olmstead. Copyright © 1977 by the author. Reprinted by permission of Harper & Row, Publishers, Inc.

"Jule Neg" (p. 97), by Pamela Krausman, adapted with permission from *Engwall's Journal,* Fall/Winter 1984.

"El Gordo" (pp. 98-100) condensed from *A Beast the Color of Winter,* by Douglas H. Chadwick. Copyright © 1983 by Douglas H. Chadwick. Reprinted with the permission of Sierra Club Books.

Excerpt from "A Christmas Memory" (pp. 106-108) copyright © 1956 by Truman Capote. Reprinted from *Selected Writings of Truman Capote,* by permission of Random House, Inc.

Condensation of "Land of December" (pp. 110-113) by Reeve L. Brown, copyright © 1978 by the National Wildlife Federation. Reprinted from the December/January 1979 issue of *National Wildlife* Magazine.

"Blizzard" (pp.126-129) condensed from *Trail of an Artist-Naturalist,* by Ernest Thompson Seton, Charles Scribner's Sons, NY, 1946. Copyright © 1940 by Ernest Thompson Seton. Reprinted by permission of Anthony Sheil Associates Ltd., London, on behalf of the Estate of Ernest Thompson Seton.

"Winter Curtain" (p. 129) reprinted from *Tallgrass Prairie: The Inland Sea,* by

Library of Congress Cataloging-in-Publication Data

Main entry under title:

National Wildlife's December treasury.

Bibliography: p.
l. Natural history—Addresses, essays, lectures. 2. Winter—Addresses, essays, lectures. 3. December—Addresses, essays, lectures. I. National Wildlife Federation. II. Title: December treasury.
QH81.N298   1985   508.73
85-15412
ISBN 0-912186-67-4

NATIONAL WILDLIFE FEDERATION

1412 16th Street, N. W.
Washington, D. C. 20036

Dr. Jay D. Hair
Executive Vice President

James D. Davis
*Senior Vice President,
Membership Development
and Publications*

STAFF FOR THIS BOOK

Howard F. Robinson
Editorial Director

Vi Kirksey
Editorial Assistant

Cecilia I. Parker
Editor

Priscilla Sharpless
Production Manager

Donna Miller
Design Director

Margaret E. Wolf
Permissions Editor

Michael E. Loomis
Judith E. Zatsick
Art Editors

Pam McCoy
Production Artist

Donna J. Reynolds
Research Editor

NATIONAL WILDLIFE FEDERATION
1412 Sixteenth Street, N.W., Washington, D.C. 20036-2266